hm
STUDY SKILLS PROGRAM
Level I

Developed by The Study Skills Group

Author: Candace Regan Burkle
                     Middlebury Union School
                     Middlebury, Vermont

Co-Author and Editor: David Marshak

Editorial Board: Kiyo Morimoto, former *Director*
                     Bureau of Study Counsel
                     Harvard University

                     Jerome A. Pieh, *Headmaster*
                     Milton Academy

                     James J. McGuinn

The National Association of Elementary School Principals
Alexandria, Virginia 22314

The National Association of Secondary School Principals
Reston, Virginia 22091

Our thanks to all of the hundreds of teachers, students, counselors, and administrators who used the first edition of the LEVEL I PROGRAM and contributed their suggestions to us.

Our deep gratitude to seven experienced and talented educators who served as revision consultants for this project and helped us to make this LEVEL I PROGRAM an even more valuable resource: NANCY BAZINET, MARGARET CAMPBELL, CAROLYN COOKE, MARJORIE DAVANZO, ELAINE FITZPATRICK, JANE HAMILTON, and NANCY HOERLE.

Illustrations by Joe Bolger

ISBN 0-88210-221-4
NASSP 987654321

TABLE OF CONTENTS

INTRODUCTION TO STUDY SKILLS

HOW DO YOU LEARN?

Not everyone learns in the same way. There are many different ways to learn. Some people like to read about something new before they try it. Other people like to learn when they can actually "do" whatever they are learning. Still others like to be told about a new thing. They like to discuss it before they try to do it. Can you think of any other ways that people learn to do new things?

The way you learn best is called your *learning style*

EXERCISE I

Directions: What do you do well? Look at the list below, and pick *one* thing that you feel you have learned to do well. Or if you prefer, pick your own activity. Write your choice on the line below.

read	cook	debate
write	play a sport	use a word processor
sail	ride a bike	play a computer game
ski	manage money	knit
play an instrument	draw	care for an animal
sew	ice skate	solve math problems

_____

Do you remember when you were learning how to do the thing you chose? If not, cross it out and pick something you remember learning.

EXERCISE II

Directions: Think about the thing you learned to do very well. How did you learn to do it?

Look at the words and phrases listed below. Circle the ones that describe how you learn best. You may also write other words and phrases that describe how you learn on the lines below.

Remember: There are no right or wrong answers! You can circle and write as many words and phrases as you need to describe how you learn.

watching	listening	doing
reading	thinking about	working when I have to
experimenting	writing	getting it right
learning from my mistakes	proving my point	"hands on"
being creative	talking it over with a friend	with a group
by myself		asking questions
looking things up	doing something I care about	
practice		

_____

_____

_____

_____

EXERCISE III

Directions: Look again at the list in EXERCISE I. This time pick out something that you've had *trouble* trying to learn well. Or if you prefer, pick your own activity. Write your choice on the line below.

_____

1. How did you try to learn the thing you said you had *trouble* learning? Look at the list in EXERCISE II again. Pick some ways that you tried to learn, and write these ways on the lines below.

_____

_____

_____

2. Have you chosen any different ways than you chose for EXERCISE II? _____

    If you answered "yes," write the different ways on the lines below.

_____

_____

_____

WHAT IS STUDY?

Some students think that "study" means just to get ready for a test. You study your spelling words Thursday night for a test on Friday. Actually, that kind of studying is only a small part of what study means.

Study means *to learn*. Whenever you are learning, you are studying, both in school and anywhere else.

Sometimes you don't think of learning as "studying" because some of the ways you learn seem to be easier than others. But whether you are trying to improve something you already do well or trying to learn something that is giving you trouble, you are studying.

Learning new words or a new kind of math problem are both studying. So are learning to sew a new stitch, play a new song, catch a high fly ball, bake a cake, or figure out a problem just by thinking about it carefully. Whenever you are trying to learn, you are studying.

WHAT ARE STUDY SKILLS?

Study skills are ways or methods of learning. They are ways of doing what you are asked to do in school that can help you to learn better. When you use study skills, you can often get more done in a given period of time and learn more, too.

Some examples of study skills are these: active listening; tuning into directions; reading for meaning; taking notes; solving problems; and preparing for tests.

HOW DO YOU LEARN STUDY SKILLS?

People learn study skills through practice. You don't learn how to play basketball by talking about the game. You have to play it. The same is true with study skills.

You often learn study skills best through the mistakes you make. Everyone makes mistakes. What's important is that you look at your mistakes carefully and find out what caused them. When you know what caused a particular mistake, you'll know how not to make that mistake again.

WHY ARE STUDY SKILLS IMPORTANT?

Learning won't suddenly become simple just because you have learned to use study skills. But these skills will help you to become a better learner. You'll probably find school more rewarding and enjoyable. You'll also be more able to learn whatever you wish outside of school.

UNIT I: WAYS TO LISTEN

LISTENING IS MORE THAN JUST HEARING

The average student spends more than half of each school day *listening*. That means that you give more time to listening than to anything else you do in school.

Most people think of listening as something as natural as walking or eating. They don't think of it as anything you have to work at to do well. But we are not *born* good listeners. We learn to be good listeners.

Why is this so? Hearing is a natural ability, but *listening* is more than just hearing. Listening means directing your attention to — or *focusing on* — what you're hearing and trying to make sense of what you've heard.

Listening is a study skill. It's one of the most important study skills because listening is a part of almost everything else that you do. It seems simple, but it's not. Being a good listener doesn't come naturally. It requires learning and practice.

WHY IS IT HARD TO LISTEN EVEN WHEN YOU'RE INTERESTED?

Generally people talk at about 125 words per minute. However, we think at a speed that is more than three times as fast, about 400 words per minute. That means our thoughts move much faster than the words of whatever we're listening to. So it's not surprising that we often let our attention wander away from what another person is saying to us.

The key to becoming a good listener is to be an *active* listener: to keep your thoughts *focused* on what you are listening to.

THE LISTENING GAME

Directions: A story will be read aloud to you only *once*. Pay close attention to the details of the story. When the story is finished, you will be asked to tell what you have heard. Listen carefully! (You are not allowed to take notes.)

WHEN YOU LISTEN, WHAT DO YOU DO?

The picture on the next page shows a classroom. It is almost the end of a class, and the teacher has given the students a few minutes to talk together. Read over their conversations.

Find the students who are called *Steve* and *Marybeth*.

Although Steve was not sitting with Marybeth's group, he heard what she had to say.

Why do you think he was able to give his attention to — or *focus on* — what Marybeth said? Write your answer on the lines below.

_____

_____

_____

_____

STEPS IN ACTIVE LISTENING

It is a *fact* that we can all become active listeners. So remember the word *FACT*. It will help you remember the steps in *active listening,* because the first letter of each of the steps spells the word *FACT*.

STEP # 1: FOCUS

The first step in active listening is to *focus*. This means to give your attention to something. Television often "catches" your attention. It doesn't require you to do the active work of *focusing*. However, when your father calls you from the next room as you are watching television, you have to pull your mind from the television to really **focus** on what he is saying.

STEP # 2: ASK

While you listen, *ask* yourself questions about what the speaker is saying. Then try to answer your questions, or see if the speaker answers them. Asking and answering questions in this way can help you make sense of the speaker's message.

When you are listening in school, you might *ask* yourself: what is it that the teacher wants me to know? Do I understand this? What don't I understand about what I am hearing? Does this make sense to me?

STEP # 3: CONNECT

Keep asking yourself why the speaker is saying what she or he is saying. Try to *connect* the main ideas with each other. For instance, the speaker may talk about growing food in a certain place. You already know that these things are needed for people to grow food: climate, soil conditions, and technology. As the speaker is talking, you will listen for and *connect* the main ideas of climate, soil conditions, and technology in order to understand how the food is grown.

STEP # 4: TRY TO PICTURE

Try to *picture in your mind* what the speaker is saying. Some people find that they can listen and remember better if they use their imaginations to make *mind pictures*. For example, if you are listening to a set of directions about how to get somewhere, make an imaginary map of the directions in your mind.

TRY IT AGAIN – THE LISTENING GAME

Directions: Again a story will be read to you only *once*. Try out the *Steps To Active Listening. Focus* on the speaker so you can pay close attention to the details of the story. *Ask* yourself how these details *connect*. Try to *picture* what is happening.

When the story is finished, you will be asked to tell what you have heard.

1. Did you find listening any easier this time? _____

   If so, why? _____

   _____

2. Which of the *Steps* is the most difficult for you to do?

   _____

   Why do you think this is so? _____

   _____

   _____

UNIT I SUMMARY: WAYS TO LISTEN

We are not born as good listeners. We have to learn to listen well. Active listening is a study skill.

We can learn to listen actively by following these steps:

Focus

> Look at the speaker. Try to pay attention to what is being said.

Ask questions

> Try to figure out what is important by asking questions. Then answer your questions, or see if the speaker answers your questions.

Connect

> "Make sense" out of what the speaker is saying by *connecting* main ideas with each other.

Try to picture

> Try to see "in your mind's eye" what the speaker is talking about.

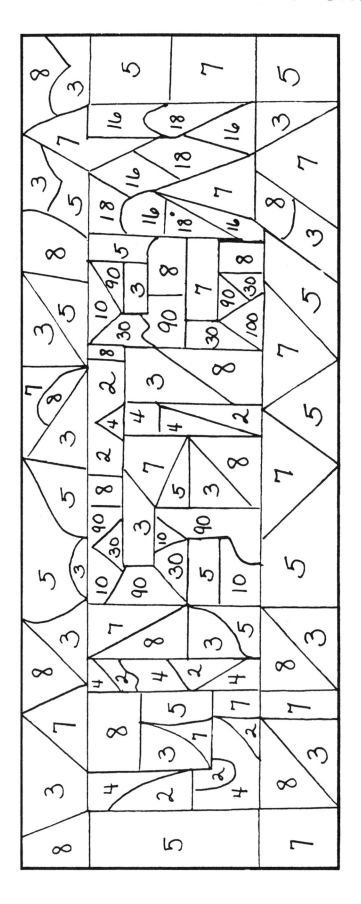

EXERCISE I

TUNING INTO DIRECTIONS

You will find that listening to and following directions is a very important skill. This is true not only in schoolwork but also in your daily life. Probably each of you has a story about a time when you only half heard or didn't hear a direction. Afterwards you found yourself in a complete mess, like the man in the old joke:

He thought they said "trains" when they passed out brains, so he ran to catch one. Never got himself a brain!

It seems that the man in the joke shares a problem with many people. Recently the students in a midwestern school received very poor grades on an achievement test. When they investigated the cause of these results, guidance counselors and classroom teachers found not poor students but poor listeners. These students had never taken this kind of test before. They weren't tuned in to listening to and following directions. So they could only guess at what they were supposed to do.

You can't guess about directions and expect to be right! You need to listen carefully and ask questions if you don't understand what you have heard.

You are already showing that you are a good listener because you are reading this page as you were instructed. Now here's an important clue! You must listen to and follow only directions #3, #7, and #9 the next time your teacher reads the directions.

The students in the midwestern school were then taught how to listen to directions. They also learned to read directions more carefully. When they took the achievement test again, they did much better. After you have read this page carefully, keep the secret to yourself! Write 3, 7, and 9 on the page before this one so you will know what directions to follow. Listen carefully, follow the right directions, and you will spell the right word in crayon.

EXERCISE II

A TOUR OF WASHINGTON, D.C.

Possible Beginnings and Ends

Lincoln Memorial – The Capitol
The Capitol — The White House
General Grant statue – Washington Monument
Botanic Gardens – The White House
Lincoln Memorial – National Art Gallery

Directions for Marking Your Map

1. Locate your beginning point. Put a star on it.

2. Locate your end point. Draw a circle around it.

3. Put an arrow above the three stops you wish to make along the way.

4. Now mark in a reasonable route. You must go down streets and avenues. Do not cross over blocks or malls.

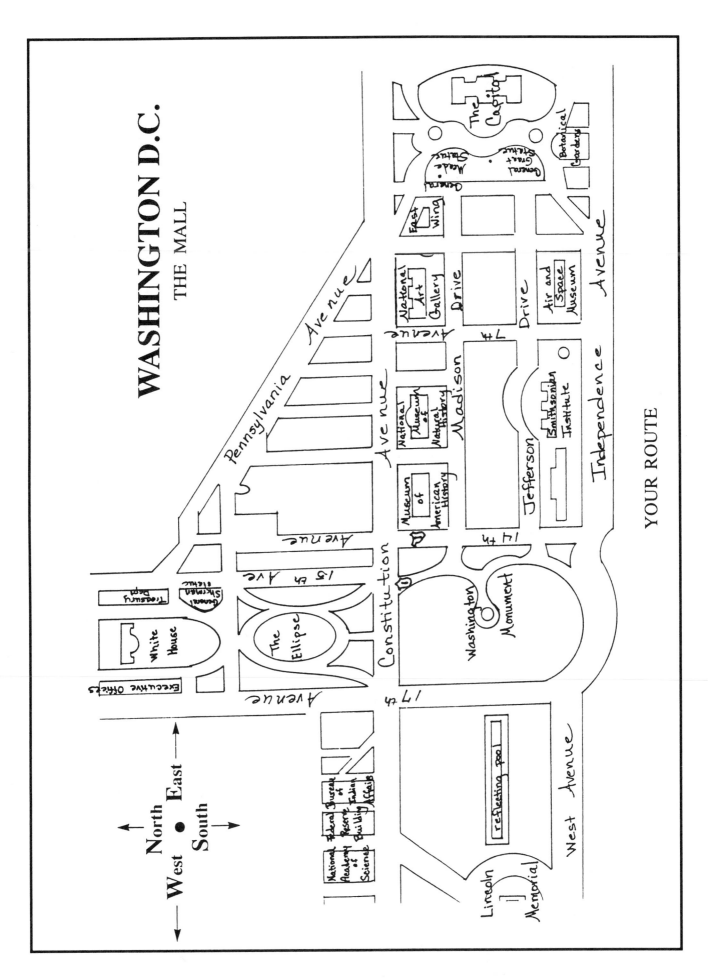

WASHINGTON D.C.
THE MALL

YOUR ROUTE

North
West • East
South

13

Giving Directions – Procedure

1. Tell your partner where to start. Have your partner mark that spot with a star.

2. Give directions to get to the first point of interest. Have your partner mark that spot with an arrow.

3. Give directions to get to your second point of interest. Have your partner mark that spot with an arrow.

4. Give directions to get to your third point of interest. Have your partner mark that spot with an arrow.

5. Give directions to get to your end spot. Have your partner mark that spot by circling it.

6. Compare maps. See how closely your routes match.

Rules and Pointers

1. All of your directions must be spoken. You may not show your map to your partner or point things out on your partner's map.

2. The listener is not allowed to say anything. This means that the listener may not ask questions or ask the speaker to repeat or wait.

3. When you are giving directions, speak slowly and clearly.

4. Use the names of roads, avenues, and streets. (Be aware that some streets are unnamed.)

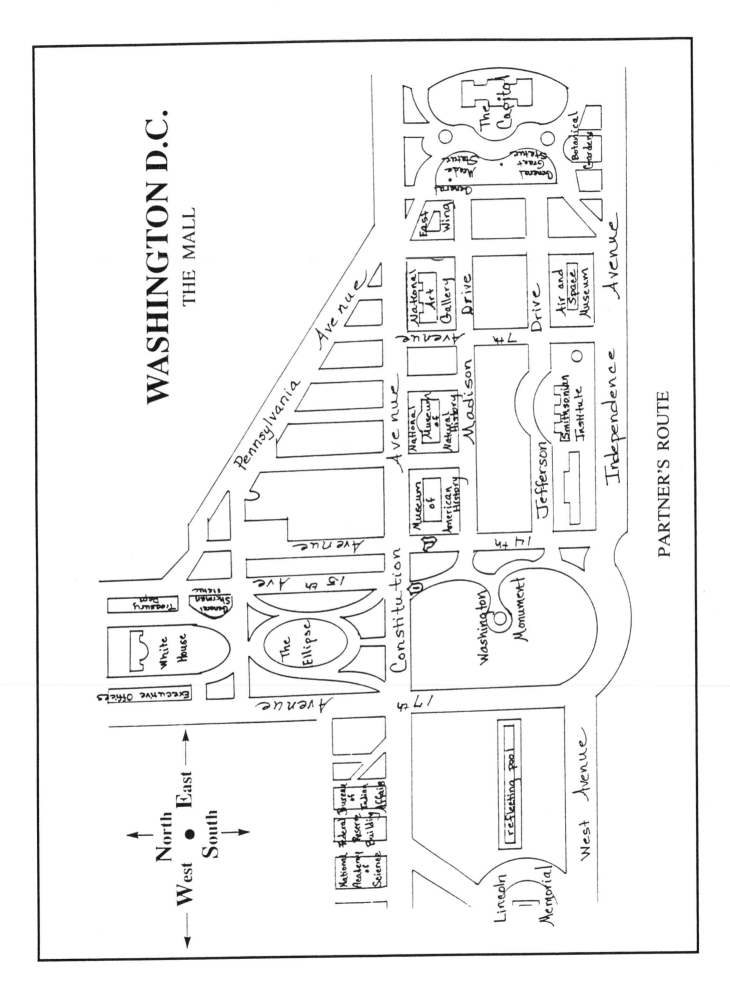

WASHINGTON D.C.
THE MALL

North
West • East
South

Pennsylvania Avenue

The Capitol

East Wing

National Art Gallery

Meade Statue

General Grant Statue

Botanical Garden

Madison Drive

Air and Space Museum

7th

Avenue

National Museum of Natural History

Independence Avenue

Museum of American History

Smithsonian Institute

Jefferson Drive

Constitution Avenue

15 th Ave

14 th

Avenue

General Sherman Statue

Treasury Dep

White House

The Ellipse

Washington Monument

Executive Offices

17 th

Avenue

National Academy of Science

Federal Reserve Building

Bureau of Indian Affairs

reflecting pool

West Avenue

Lincoln Memorial

PARTNER'S ROUTE

15

UNIT II SUMMARY: TUNING INTO DIRECTIONS

Remember the STEPS IN ACTIVE LISTENING from Unit I. They are these:

Focus

Look at the speaker. Try to pay attention to what is being said.

Ask questions

Try to figure out what is important by asking questions. Then answer your questions, or see if the speaker answers your questions.

Connect

Make sense out of what the speaker is saying by *connecting* main ideas with each other.

Try to picture

Try to see *in your mind's eye* what the speaker is talking about.

Reading and listening to directions is an important skill. This is true not only in school but in any situation in life.

Read directions carefully. Be sure to read *all* of the directions. Then if you don't understand, ask questions. If you are not allowed to ask questions, ask yourself the questions and listen for the answers.

Listen carefully when someone is giving you directions. Don't try to guess what they are. Listen to *all* of the directions. Then if you don't understand what you've heard, ask questions.

If you can't remember all the directions, write them down on a piece of paper.

UNIT III: GETTING THE TIMING DOWN

INTRODUCTION

When you read or hear a story, you can understand it better if you know the order in which the events are taking place. Knowing the order of events means that you know what happened first, what happened next, and so on.

Another way of saying this is that you know the *sequence* of events. The *sequence* is the order in which the events take place.

"Getting the timing down" means to understand the sequence of events in a story. Sometimes people call "getting the timing down" by another name: *sequencing*.

The exercises in this unit will help you learn more about "getting the timing down" or *sequencing*.

EXERCISE I

PHILIP'S STORY: WHAT'S THE SEQUENCE OF EVENTS?

Directions: Read the paragraphs below, and follow all of the underlined instructions.

On the next page, you'll find a map of Philip's neighborhood. Philip lives in the last house on the right side of Torrey Ave. as you are heading west. *Mark his house so you can see where he lives.*

Philip has many errands to do, and he only has a short time before he has to pick up his sister, Anne, at the day care center.

Below you'll find a list of Philip's errands. *First read over all of the errands.* You can use your map as a reference as you read them. *Then figure out in what sequence Philip should do his errands so he can do them as quickly as possible.* Marking the map in pencil may be helpful to you.

When you have decided on a sequence, number the errands below so they will show the sequence of events. In the space on the left of each errand, mark the first errand #1, the second #2, and so on.

A. _____ Philip is hungry. He buys a double scoop pistachio and chocolate ice cream cone at CHUCK'S.

B. _____ Philip wants to see "A Day In The Life Of Alfred E. Newman," which is playing at the THEATER tonight. He stops to buy two tickets.

C. _____ Philip takes his little sister, Anne, to DONNA'S KENNELS to look at the puppies.

D. _____ Philip decides to ride his bike so he can do everything faster. The tires need air. Before he can do anything else, he goes to F.B. GARAGE to fill his tires.

E. _____ Philip brings Anne home. He turns on the stereo and relaxes. It's been a long afternoon, but it's all over now.

F. _____ Philip wants to play Little League this year, so he stops to register at WELLINGTON FIELD. He notices the theater's billboard across the street.

G. _____ Philip has to pick up his little sister, Anne, at C.T.'s DAYCARE. Anne begs to see the puppies at Donna's Kennels.

H. _____ Philip drops two overdue books off at the LIBRARY. He doesn't go in to pay for them because he still has ice cream on his hands.

I. _____ DORIE'S COOKIE FACTORY sells day-old cookies at half price. Philip's mother wants him to pick up a pound of cookies, so he does.

PHILIP'S NEIGHBORHOOD

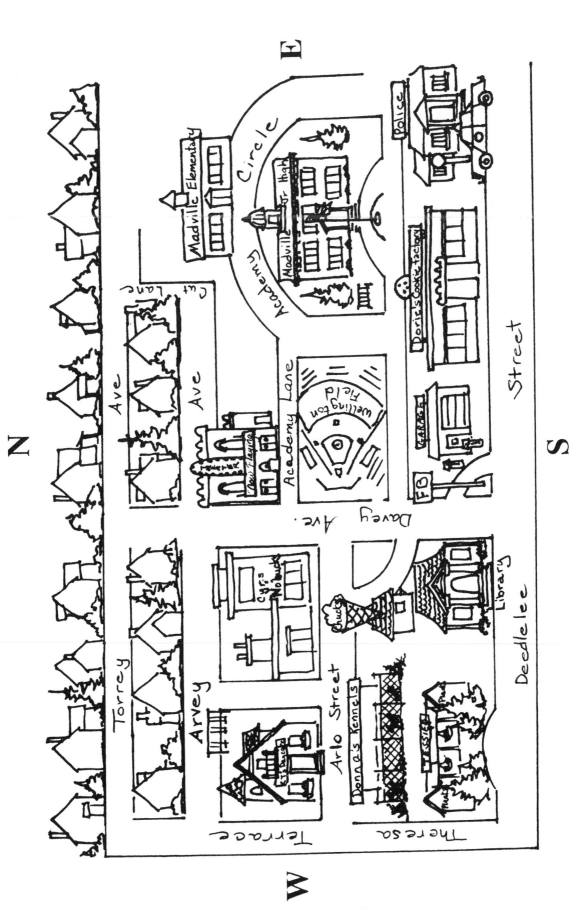

KEY WORDS: TIME QUALIFIERS

When you read or listen to a story, you will often find key words that can give you an idea about *when* events in the story take place. These key words are *time qualifiers*. These words qualify other words or phrases. To qualify is to make the meaning of words or phrases clearer.

Some examples of *time qualifiers* that tell you more about when events take place are these:

while	during	before
after	as	until
following	afterwards	in the meantime

There are many other *time qualifiers*. Any word or phrase that helps you to understand when events are happening is a *time qualifier*.

EXERCISE II

Directions: Each of the sentences below includes two events. In each sentence, circle the word(s) that you recognize as a *time qualifier*. Then underline the event that happens first.

If the events in a sentence are happening at the same time, do not underline anything.

EXAMPLES

Before Molly left for school, she ate two pieces of toast.

We set up the tents while the others gathered firewood.

1. I had a great time after I got to know all of the people there.

2. Before Miguel had realized the danger he was in, he was enjoying sailing over the wild waves.

3. Darcy searched for clues to the disappearance of her brother, Ted, but in the meantime, he slept soundly, unaware that she was trying to find him.

4. It had taken years of hard work, but finally the statue was finished.

5. Following the wedding ceremony, there was a reception at the Martin Luther King Community Center.

6. Water expands when it is cooled.

7. As the ice masses drew back, they carved lakes and hills upon the earth's surface.

8. Divide the money equally among yourselves, and then go to the store.

9. All during the time I had been outdoors planting, the baby had been playing happily in her pen.

10. The water pressure built up until the dam finally cracked.

FINDING CLUES TO THE TIMING

Sometimes the events described in a story are not in a sequence. The author may tell one part of the story and then jump into the past or the future. When an author jumps around in time like this, she or he must give clues to help the reader understand what is happening. Often these clues are *time qualifiers*.

When you are reading or listening to a story, pay attention to the *time qualifiers*. They can help you understand what happened and when it happened. This helps you to follow the story better.

EXERCISE III

Directions: In the story below, underline the time qualifiers. Then number the events listed on page 24 in the order in which they happened. Number the first event #1, the second event #2, and so on.

The skies were heavy with thick gray clouds. It was only three o'clock. Still early, Nick thought, he'd have plenty of time to get home. Earlier this morning Nick had listened to the weather report. The weather people had predicted a major snowstorm. From the looks of the sky, he was sure that the prediction would come true.

Nick was excited. He loved the snow. The prospect of walking home in the snowstorm bothered him not at all. He was well bundled and had just a little less than a mile to go. The path through the woods was completely clear. If it did snow, it would be the first snow of the season.

After Nick had been walking for about ten minutes, thick flakes began to swirl around him. Long ago, when he was in preschool, his teacher had told the class that each flake that fell from the sky was different. Ever since then, Nick had tried to find two flakes that were exactly alike, He hadn't found them yet, but he was sure that of the millions that fell from the sky, if he kept looking, he would find the magical pair. He'd always told himself that when he found them, he would get whatever he'd wish for.

Nick was so busy catching and examining the lovely flakes that he didn't notice that the storm was intensifying. The swirling flakes had gathered force. The forest path was now a line of white winding through the tall pines. But Nick was not concentrating on the gathering forces of the snow. He was mesmerized by the thought of finding the two identical flakes. He stopped in his favorite spot, a clearing beneath two sycamore trees, so that he would have more light to examine the snow.

By the time he gave some attention to what was happening around him, the snow had become thick. It was so thick, in fact, that he could barely make out the outline of the trees around the clearing. He became a bit alarmed as he remembered his mother telling him, "Nick, this will be our first winter here. The storms in these parts come up quickly. You don't get the same warning as we did back east. Soon the ground is covered, and you can't see your hand in front of your face."

At the time Nick thought his mother was being a bit over-cautious. Not even here in the midwest could a storm sneak up that quickly on a boy who had experienced snowstorms all his life. But as Nick searched for the path that should now continue through a grove of maples, he knew his mother had been right to warn him.

Continued on page 24.

23

Still he wasn't worried. He was very close to home after all, and the snow was just beginning to cover the ground. He did, however, quicken his pace. In his haste and because the snow made the forest a new, strange world, Nick took the wrong turn. He had gone half a mile when he discovered that he was heading toward the pond, not the old farmhouse that his family had moved into last summer.

The storm was lashing out in all its fury. Nick couldn't see the nose in front of his face, much less his hand. The maple and ash trees no longer protected the winding path. Now Nick was worried. He raced in what he thought was the right direction. It was getting dark. Soon he would not even have the comfort of daylight.

"Whatever am I going to do?" thought Nick as he admitted to himself that he didn't know if he was heading home or in some wild circle towards the pond. He was growing tired, and he realized that he'd have to catch his breath and think clearly before going on. He pulled his parka away from his watch to see how much time he would have left before total darkness was upon him. Instead of looking at his watch, he saw, wide-eyed, two snow flakes that for all the world looked perfectly alike. Here was the chance to test his theory.

"Oh, I wish I could find my way home!"

Just then, his dog, Monster, bounded into his arms. He was a great German shepherd with an amazing sense of direction. Nick knew now he had found his way home.

a. _____ Nick's family moved from the East.

b. _____ The weather people had predicted a snowstorm.

c. _____ Nick's mother had warned him about midwestern snowstorms.

d. _____ Nick's preschool teacher had told him no two snowflakes were alike.

e. _____ The storm was intensifying.

f. _____ Nick noticed the powerful storm.

g. _____ Nick was looking for a pair of identical snowflakes.

h. _____ It was three o'clock in the afternoon.

i. _____ Nick's dog, Monster, found him.

j. _____ Nick had taken the wrong turn.

PREDICTING OUTCOMES

When you are reading or listening to a story, you can use *time qualifiers* to help you understand the sequence of events. Then when you know what has already happened, you can often figure out what will happen next in the story.

Figuring out what will probably happen next is called *predicting outcomes*. When you predict an outcome, you use what you already know about a story to make a "good guess" about what will happen next.

Trying to *predict outcomes* also helps you to become actively involved in whatever you're hearing or reading.

When you predict an outcome, you ask yourself questions and try to answer them before you read or are told what happens.

EXERCISE IV

Directions:　Read the paragraphs below and on pages 26-27. Circle the *time qualifiers* that help you to think about the possible outcome of each story. Then answer the question(s) that follows each paragraph.

1.　When I awoke this morning, the sun was shining brightly in a clear, blue sky. I was excited because this was the day I had planned for the big picnic. After breakfast I turned on the radio and heard the weather report: "A moist cold front will be traveling rapidly across the Pacific Northwest. This front will push out the high currently settled over our region and will bring heavy rain. Rains will continue into tomorrow..." When I looked at the mountain to the west, I saw billowing black clouds.

Do you think this person will have a picnic on this day? What makes you think this?

_____

_____

_____

_____

2. My teacher asked me to do an experiment to prove that a vacuum, or empty space, can't exist if there is something available to fill it. I knew that a candle needed oxygen to burn, and I also knew that oxygen took up space. So I put a candle in a shallow bowl and put an inch of water into the bowl. When I put a glass jar over the candle, I knew the candle would go out after it had used up all the oxygen within the jar. Then, with all the oxygen gone, the empty space within the jar would need to be filled, if possible, with another substance.

Predict what will happen to the water in the bowl. Explain your prediction.

_____

_____

_____

3. They say that if you don't learn from your mistakes, then "history will repeat itself." I never knew what that meant until I figured out there was a reason why I kept turning up on the "lost list." The first time I got lost, I had an excuse: I was only five years old. My mother had said, "Stay right here while Mama tries this dress on." I didn't listen to her. Instead I followed a cart full of toys. I should have learned to listen from that experience, but I didn't. I was seven when the teacher told our class to report to the auditorium after lunch. Again I wasn't listening, so I spent the better part of the afternoon looking for my class. When it finally came time for our class trip to Montreal, I was really excited. I was also determined not to get lost, but as I said, "History has a way of repeating itself."

Do you think the writer gets lost in Montreal? Why do you think the way you do?

_____

_____

_____

4. In 1641 the population of New France was 240. Most of the people living there were single soldiers. French officials asked unmarried women to come to the New World to become soldiers' wives. Ships soon arrived in New France carrying more than 150 female immigrants. Then the government offered special rewards for large families. If people had ten children, they received a pension. Girls were given large sums if they married before they were sixteen. Boys who married before the age of twenty also received special rewards.

Predict the population of New France in 1675. What makes you think this?

_____

_____

_____

_____

UNIT III SUMMARY: GETTING THE TIMING DOWN

"Getting the timing down" means understanding the order of events in a story. The order in which things take place in a story is also called the *sequence* of events.

When you read or listen to a story, you can recognize key words that tell you about when events take place. These words are called *time qualifiers*. Some examples of time qualifiers are these: after, before, until, while, following, during.

You can use your ability to "get the timing down" to understand when things happen in a story and to *predict outcomes*. This means to use what you already know about the sequence of events in a story to figure out what will probably happen next. By trying to predict outcomes as you read or listen, you can become a more active and involved reader or listener.

UNIT IV: A MATTER OF TIME

INTRODUCTION

Think about the meaning of the word *time*. Can you give a definition for this word? Does this word have more than one meaning for you?

Write your definition for the word *time* on the lines below. If you can think of more than one definition, write two or three.

time: _____

_____

_____

_____

_____

_____

You may have found it difficult to define the word *time*. Time is not something that we can touch, see, or smell. Yet we can "feel" time or sense it as it passes. And we can also "hear" time or sense the order in a piece of music.

Our sense of time seems to change as we grow older. For instance, now you'd probably think that you're wasting your time if you were perfectly healthy and spent a whole day in bed. When you were a baby, however, you were usually content to lie in bed, asleep and awake, for most of the day and night.

This unit will help you to look more carefully at what time is and how you use your time.

EXERCISE I

Directions: Look at the time line on the next page. Start with the first column. Fill in the year you were born under YEAR. Also fill in the other years.

Next read through the events listed below.

Match the events to the time line according to what has happened in *your* life.

Write each event in the appropriate space under the heading marked EVENTS IN MY LIFE.

You may not remember some events clearly. Make a good guess about when they occurred. Just do your best to remember. There are no right or wrong answers.

I started school.

I began to read books by myself.

I got my first tooth.

I had a nightmare that I can still remember.

I entered fourth grade.

I had my most memorable birthday.

I learned how to print.

I first met the person who is now my best friend.

I rode a bicycle for the first time.

TIME LINE: MY LIFE

YEAR	YEAR IN MY LIFE	EVENTS IN MY LIFE
	0	I was born.
	1	
	2	
	3	
	4	
	5	
	6	
	7	
	8	
	9	I was nine years old.
	10	
	11	
	12	
	13	
	14	
	15	
	16	
	17	

Now put a star in front of each event that you think happened in the lives of all the other people in your class during the same YEAR IN MY LIFE. (It does not have to be the same calendar YEAR.)

EXERCISE II

Directions: Sometimes it's important for us to know if events happened before or after other events.

Arrange each group of events below according to when you think they happened. Which happened first? Put a #1 in the blank before the event that happened first. Put a #2 in the blank before the event that happened next, and so on up to #4.

REMEMBER: The event that happened first is the one that took place *the longest time ago*.

GROUP A

_____ Television was invented.

_____ Radio was invented.

_____ The personal computer was invented.

_____ The horse-drawn wagon was invented.

GROUP B

_____ My mother was born.

_____ Columbus sailed to America.

_____ The automobile was invented.

_____ The last of the dinosaurs died out.

GROUP C

_____ People first invented language.

_____ George Washington was elected the first President of the United States.

_____ The Egyptians built the pyramids.

_____ My teacher was born.

A STRING OF EVENTS – PLANNING THE STEPS

When you have a certain project in mind such as making a shirt, building a shelf, or getting a book report ready for school, you often think backwards. In other words, you imagine what needs to be done first. Then you think about what you need to do to get the project done.

For instance, if you want to do your book report, you think about all the things that need to be done before you can write a final draft. Some of those things might be:

read the book
discuss the book with your teacher
outline the main events
outline the main characters
write a rough draft

You must have a clear idea of the project you wish to do. You must also think of the steps you need to take in order to get this project done. It is helpful to think of these steps as *a string of events*. In other words, all the steps you take and the order in which you take them must have a logical connection. You can't outline the main events of the book until you have read the book.

EXERCISE III

Directions: Look at the Example below and events 1-3 on page 34. The steps that are listed below them are not in the correct order.

Suggest a better order by numbering the first thing to be done as #1, and the second thing as #2, and so on.

Example

Make pancakes

a. _____ mix ingredients
b. _____ heat skillet
c. _____ read recipe
d. _____ eat pancakes
e. _____ find recipe
f. _____ get out necessary ingredients
g. _____ put mixture in hot, greased skillet
h. _____ flip pancakes

1. Change the tire on my bicycle

a. _____ take out the old tube
b. _____ blow up the new tube
c. _____ check inside of the tire for anything that might puncture new tube
d. _____ take off tire
e. _____ put in new tube
f. _____ put tire back on

2. Make a stuffed pillow

a. _____ sew the pieces together
b. _____ fill the pillow with polyester fill
c. _____ pick out a design
d. _____ cut out the pattern pieces
e. _____ pick out the materials
f. _____ leave an open seam for filling
g. _____ stitch up open seam

3. Plan to see a movie

a. _____ call friend
b. _____ check available movies in the newspaper
c. _____ suggest going to a movie together
d. _____ check to see if I have enough money
e. _____ get permission from parents
f. _____ arrange transportation
g. _____ go to see movie

EXERCISE IV

Directions: Now look at the tasks below and on page 36. Create a string of events for doing the tasks below. Write the events on the lines provided.

Example

Make a bacon, lettuce, and tomato sandwich

1. check to see if I have ingredients
2. fry the bacon
3. wash the lettuce-set it on towel to dry
4. cut tomatoes
5. drain fat from bacon
6. toast bread
7. put mayonnaise on toast
8. layer the bacon, lettuce, and tomato on toast
9. put on top of sandwich
10. cut sandwich in half
11. eat

Make a paper mache mask

_____

_____

_____

_____

_____

_____

_____

_____

_____

Put a young child to bed

_____

_____

_____

_____

_____

_____

_____

_____

Study for a spelling quiz

_____

_____

_____

_____

_____

_____

_____

_____

WHAT IS A SCHEDULE?

As you grow older, you begin to think more about the "string" of events in your life: what will happen tomorrow, and the next day, and so on. As you do, you'll want to be able to plan some of the events ahead of time.

When you are trying to plan ahead, it can be helpful to make a *schedule* for yourself. A *schedule is a plan for what you want to do in the future.*

Usually when you plan, you "string" things that need to happen backwards. That is, *first* you decide what your goal is. Then you figure out how you can reach it.

For instance, you might be thinking of the goal of having a Friday evening pizza party. The pizza party is the last thing that will happen in the string. Some of the steps you have to take before the party are these:

ask your parents for permission
save your allowance
invite your friends
buy the paper goods
buy drinks
clean the party room
borrow some tapes to play
order the pizza
pick up the pizza

When you do this kind of planning, a *schedule* helps you to understand what the steps are to reach your goal and when you need to do them. Look at the sample *schedule* on page 38 for *Planning My Pizza Party*.

WEEKLY SCHEDULE	Day 1 Saturday	Day 2 Sunday	Day 3 Monday	Day 4 Tuesday	Day 5 Wednesday	Day 6 Thursday	Day 7 Friday
Morning — Before School	Ask parents for Permission						
Mid-Day — During School			Invite friends that I didn't call	Ask friends to bring tapes			
Late Afternoon — After School	Babysit to earn money	Call friends to invite them	Get allowance DON'T SPEND IT!	Call friends I didn't see to bring tapes		Go Shopping: paper goods other munchies drinks cups	Set up for party Order Pizza Pick up Pizza
Evening — After Dinner						Clean party room	PARTY!

Schedule for Planning My Pizza Party

38

EXERCISE V

MAKING A SCHEDULE

Directions: 1. Choose something you would really like to do from the goals listed below, or think of your own goal.

Circle the goal of your choice if it's one of the goals listed below. If it isn't, write your goal on the line below the list.

learn a computer program

plan a _____ party

get a book report done

get a school project done

make a new friend

build a model (airplane, car, boat, etc.)

finish a sewing project

My goal is _____

2. Now make a list of steps – or a string of events – that have to be done before your goal is accomplished.

_____

_____

_____

_____

_____

_____

_____

_____

_____

Continued on page 40.

3. On *My Schedule* on page 41, write tomorrow's day of the week in the blank below Day 1. Then write in the rest of the days of the week on your schedule.

4. Think about when you want to do the first step that you have listed above. When you have decided when to do that step, write the step into the correct box on *My Schedule*. Do the same for all the other steps that lead to your goal. *BE SURE TO WRITE YOUR SCHEDULE IN PENCIL!* If you write in pencil, you'll be able to make changes in your schedule if you need to do so.

    REMEMBER: When you plan to work on your project during a block of time, that doesn't mean you'll spend all of that time working on your project. It means you'll spend at least some time on your project.

    For example, let's say that you plan to work on a step during Tuesday evening after dinner and write that into your schedule. This means that you intend to spend at least some time on your step during Tuesday evening.

5. When you have finished making your schedule for the goal you have chosen, look carefully at what you have planned. Does it seem reasonable to you? Is this a plan that will work for you? If not, change it.

WEEKLY SCHEDULE	Day 1	Day 2	Day 3	Day 4	Day 5	Day 6	Day 7
Morning — Before School							
Mid-Day — During School							
Late Afternoon — After School							
Evening — After Dinner							

My Schedule

USING YOUR SCHEDULE: WHAT HAPPENED?

How well did your schedule work for you? Think about the questions below, and then answer them.

1. Did I get everything done that I wanted to do?

   _____

2. Did anything get in the way of my schedule? If things did get in the way, what were they?

   _____

   _____

   _____

3. How could I make a more useful schedule?

   _____

   _____

4. How does making plans seem helpful to me?

   _____

   _____

5. How does making plans seem not helpful to me?

   _____

   _____

UNIT IV SUMMARY: A MATTER OF TIME

Making a *schedule* for yourself can be helpful when you're trying to plan ahead. A *schedule* is a plan for what you want to do in the future.

When you're making a schedule, first think about what you want to do or the goal you want to accomplish. Then think about all the steps you have to take to reach that goal.

Write into your schedule *when* you plan to work and *what* you plan to get done each time that you work.

When you finish making your schedule, look it over carefully. Does it seem reasonable for you? If not, change it.

After you use your schedule, think about how well it worked for you. Was your schedule helpful? If it wasn't helpful, how could you make a more useful schedule?

UNIT V: PUTTING IDEAS TOGETHER

EXERCISE I

Directions: List all of the words that you can remember from the list of words your teacher gave you.

_____	_____	_____	_____
_____	_____	_____	_____
_____	_____	_____	_____
_____	_____	_____	_____
_____	_____	_____	_____

Directions: Try it again. This time you will have looked at a list that has been organized differently.

_____	_____	_____	_____
_____	_____	_____	_____
_____	_____	_____	_____
_____	_____	_____	_____
_____	_____	_____	_____

WHY DO YOU ORGANIZE INFORMATION?

When you organize information or ideas, you can discover how the various pieces of information or ideas relate to each other. Also you can usually remember information and ideas better when you organize them.

HOW DO YOU ORGANIZE INFORMATION?

Each word in the lists that your teacher gave you is a piece of information. Each time you tried the exercise above, half of you had a list in which the words were organized into *categories*.

A *category* is a name for a group of ideas or pieces of information that have something in common. For example, *birds* is a category. Duck, hen, robin, swan, and raven all fit into the category of *birds*.

Putting ideas and information into categories is a good way to organize your ideas and information. It will help you to remember them better and to understand how the ideas and information are similar and how they are different.

EXAMPLE

Directions: Look at the following group of words. Then answer the questions below it.

Louisiana	Toronto	New Jersey
Los Angeles	New Mexico	New York

1. Which word(s) fits into the category of *cities*?_____

   _____

2. Which word(s) fits into the category of *words ending in vowels*? _____

   _____

3. Which word(s) does *not* fit into the category of places in the United States?

   _____

4. Name a category in which all of these words fit.

   _____

EXERCISE II

Directions: Look at the words in Group A. Then answer the questions below it. Do the same for Groups B–D on pages 47-49.

GROUP A

ocean	lake	stream
river	mountain	sea

1. Which word(s) fits into the category of *bodies of water*? _____

    _____

2. Which word(s) can *not* be listed in the category of *words beginning with consonants*?

    _____

    _____

3. Which word(s) can be listed in the category of *items found on a map of your state*?

    _____

    _____

4. Name a category in which all of these words fit.

    _____

GROUP B

wet	cold	green
dark	dry	hot

5. Which word(s) probably fits into the category of *words used to describe a desert*?

   _____

6. Which word(s) probably fits into the category of *words used to describe winter at the North Pole*?

   _____

7. Which word(s) fits into the category of *words that describe temperatures*?

   _____

8. Name a category in which all of these words fit.

   _____

GROUP C

empress	doctor	king
president	mechanic	pilot

9. Which word(s) fits into the category of *occupations that only women can have?*

_____

10. Which word(s) fits into the category of *occupations that only men can have?*

_____

11. Which word(s) can *not* be found in the category of *leaders of countries?*

_____

12. Name a category in which all of these words fit.

_____

GROUP D

roots	stems	plants
leaves	seeds	green

13. Which word(s) does *not* fit into the category of *parts of plants*? _____

_____

14. Which word(s) fits into the category of *colors*? _____

_____

15. Which word(s) does *not* fit into the category of *words that have two vowels together that make a single sound*?

_____

_____

16. Name a category in which *none* of these words fits.

_____

EXERCISE III

Directions: Look at the words in Group E. Then answer the questions below it. Do the same for Groups F-L on pages 50-56.

For Groups H-L on pages 52-56, list the letters of phrases or sentences that you choose. You don't need to copy the phrase or sentence itself.

GROUP E

gasoline	wood	coal
water	air	steel

17.   Which word(s) fits into the category of *things that will burn?* _____

_____

18.   Which word(s) fits into the category of *liquids?* _____

_____

19.   Which word(s) fits into the category of *metals?* _____

_____

20.   Name a category in which all of these words fit.

_____

GROUP F

heart	feather	skin
fur	lung	scales

21.   Which word(s) fits into the category of *things that are inside the bodies of animals?*

_____

22.   Which word(s) fits into the category of *coverings that protect animals?*

_____

23.   Which word(s) does *not* fit into the category of *parts of animals?*

_____

24.   Name *two* categories in which all of these words fit.

_____

GROUP G

| fraction | subtraction | addition |
| multiplication | calculator | computer |

25. Which word(s) does *not* fit into the category of *mathematical terms*?

   _____

26. Which word(s) does *not* fit into the category of *machines*?

   _____

27. Which word(s) fits into the category of *words that have at least four syllables*?

   _____

28. Name two categories in which none of these words fits.

   _____

GROUP H

a. go to the store
b. mend the cuffs
c. fix bathroom faucet
d. pick up laundry
e. call Jane
f. write letters

29. Which phrase(s) fits into the category of *chores*? _____

_____

30. Which phrase(s) fits into the category of *errands*? _____

_____

31. Which phrase(s) fits into the category of *things to do in my free time*?

_____

32. Name a category in which all of these phrases fit.

_____

GROUP I

a. once upon a time
b. this little piggy
c. Christopher Robin
d. who's been sleeping in my bed?
e. not by the hair of my chinny chin chin
f. the little red hen

33. Which phrase(s) fits into the category of *characters from children's tales?*

_____

34. Which phrase(s) fits into the category of *well known lines?*

_____

35. Which phrase(s) fits into the category of *dialogue* (the words characters speak)?

_____

36. Name a category in which all of these phrases fit.

_____

GROUP J

a. examining animal characteristics and behavior
b. analyzing data gathered from telescope observation
c. finding cures for diseases
d. writing observations
e. collecting information
f. studying climate

37. Which phrase(s) fits into the category of *parts of a scientist's job?* _____

    _____

38. Which phrase(s) fits into the category of *ways that meteorologists* (scientists who study the weather) *make predictions?*

    _____

    _____

39. Which phrase(s) fits into the category of *part of an animal behaviorist's job?*

    _____

40. Name a category in which all of these phrases fit.

    _____

GROUP K

a. A small cottage stood alone in the dark woods.
b. King Midas wished that everything he touched would turn to gold.
c. The fox kept praising Chanticleer.
d. Midas's daughter was unaware that everything her father touched would turn to gold.
e. Chanticleer was a rooster who was overly proud of himself.
f. This pride eventually got the vain bird in trouble.
g. King Midas's beautiful castle and many riches were not enough.

41. Which sentence(s) fits into the category called "The Golden Touch"?

    _____

42. Which sentence(s) fits into the category called "The Fox and Chanticleer"?

    _____

43. Which sentence(s) fits into neither category?

    _____

44. Name a category in which all of these sentences fit.

    _____

GROUP L

a. Several Indian or Native American tribes populated the continent of North America before the arrival of white people.
b. When the Europeans invaded South America, they found many highly developed Native American civilizations.
c. The North American Indian tribes formed seven nations.
d. One of the most highly developed South American tribes was the Incas.
e. The Algonquin was one great Native American nation of Northeastern America.
f. The Inca tribe of South America was a part of a larger branch called the Quecha.
g. The Delaware tribe inhabited the region where Pennsylvania is today.

45. Which sentence(s) fits into the category of *Native Americans of North America*?

_____

46. Which sentence(s) fits into the category of *South American Native Americans*?

_____

47. Which of the sentences above would *not* fit into a category of Columbus's voyages?

_____

48. Name a category in which all of these sentences fit.

_____

EXERCISE IV

Directions: Organize the words below into as many categories as possible.

List the categories and the words grouped within them in the spaces below and on the following pages. You must list at least three words in each category that you create. You may use the same word in more than one category.

Try to create categories that no one else will!

star	see	lobster	crow
man	walnut	treasure	creator
wave	stove	woman	October
July	fox	mountain	pocket
loon	September	drummer	potato
cashew	strawberry	highway	volcano
earthquake	ax	hammer	hyena
empress	meteor	goat	stew
dunce	sponge	August	rat
octopus	river	ostrich	crater
wedge	June	saw	stone
fish	earth	ribbon	drill
valley	eel	November	onion
canary	hill	rake	whale

CATEGORY _____

Words _____

_____

_____

_____

CATEGORY _____

Words _____

_____

_____

_____

CATEGORY _____

Words _____

_____

_____

_____

CATEGORY _____

Words _____

_____

_____

_____

CATEGORY _____

Words _____

_____

_____

_____

CATEGORY _____

Words _____

_____

_____

_____

CATEGORY _____

Words _____

_____

_____

_____

CATEGORY _____

Words _____

_____

_____

_____

CATEGORY _____

Words _____

_____

_____

_____

CATEGORY _____

Words _____

_____

_____

_____

CATEGORY _____

Words _____

_____

_____

_____

CATEGORY _____

Words _____

_____

_____

_____

CATEGORY _____

Words _____

_____

_____

_____

CATEGORY _____

Words _____

_____

_____

_____

CATEGORY _____   CATEGORY _____

Words _____   Words _____

_____   _____

_____   _____

_____   _____

CATEGORY _____   CATEGORY _____

Words _____   Words _____

_____   _____

_____   _____

_____   _____

CATEGORY _____   CATEGORY _____

Words _____   Words _____

_____   _____

_____   _____

_____   _____

CATEGORY _____   CATEGORY _____

Words _____   Words _____

_____   _____

_____   _____

_____   _____

UNIT V SUMMARY: PUTTING IDEAS TOGETHER

A category is a name for a group of ideas or pieces of information that have something in common.

For example, city, state, town and village all fit into the category of *units of government.*

When you organize ideas and information into categories, you can usually remember them better. Also you will discover how ideas and information are similar and how they are different.

CHALLENGE

Directions: Study the picture on page 60. Imagine yourself in this part of this city. Your teacher will give you some suggestions for imagining. Listen to them first. Then try the four challenges below.

1. Imagine that you are at Point A, at the top of the building looking down at the city below. Describe what you see to your partner.

2. Now in your mind's eye, go across the street to Point B. Tell your partner how the city looks from this viewpoint. What things are different? What things are the same?

3. Now you are down the street at Point C. Imagine what the city looks like from here. Describe what you see to your partner.

4. Try imagining that you are sitting in a car at Point D. Look out the window, and tell your partner how you see things differently.

INTRODUCTION

The first two units in this *Program* asked you to picture things in your mind's eye. You are probably better at this than you realize. If you could picture or imagine any details about the picture of page 60, then you already picture things in your mind quite well. If that task was difficult for you, you have probably imagined a solution to a problem such as how to build a model, sew pieces together to make clothes, or take a short cut through the neighborhood. Also you can probably close your eyes right now and, in your mind's eye, see your teacher's face. Doing any of these tasks shows that you are able to imagine or picture things in your mind's eye.

You may not have thought that this ability to picture or imagine could help you with your school work. However, picturing is an important study skill. Picturing in your mind's eye can help you be an active listener, remember details, and solve problems. In this unit you will learn about some of the ways that picturing can help you.

PICTURES IN YOUR MIND: ACTIVE LISTENING

EXERCISE 1

Directions: Your teacher is going to read a short story to you. As your teacher reads the story, try to imagine or picture details in your mind. After the story is finished, you will be asked to answer some questions about what things in the story look like.

***NOTE:** While you're listening, try to get comfortable, so that you can really picture the details. If it helps, you can close your eyes.

1. Was the sun shining? _____

2. What does Mindy look like? What color hair does she have? How tall is she? What color eyes does she have?

_____

_____

_____

_____

3. What color hair does Harriet have? What is she wearing? _____

_____

4. Did you picture buildings other than the coffee shop, the church, and Mademoiselle's? What did they look like? Were the buildings shops? Offices? Restaurants?

_____

_____

_____

5. What kind of a shop is Mademoiselle's? _____

_____

6. Can you imagine the coat Mindy has on? What color is it? What material is it made from?

_____

_____

_____

7. Can you imagine the dress Mindy has on? What color is it? Does it have long sleeves or short sleeves?

_____

_____

_____

Continued on page 64.

8. Describe the church across the street. How big is it? What material is it made from? Does it have any windows?

_____

_____

_____

_____

9. Does the street have any traffic? _____

_____

10. What does Mindy's father look like? _____

_____

_____

The city's skyline seemed to reach down and choke Mindy. She looked for something familiar, but all she saw was a blur of faces and the drab color of winter clothes as a rush of human bodies pushed her aside. She would have liked to have gone into the coffee shop. She was standing right in front of it. It looked so inviting with its neatly set tables and windows full of plants. But if she went in, she might not see her father who was supposed to be here at two o'clock.

"Are you lost, little girl?"

Mindy looked up alarmed. The face peering at her was not an unkind one. The woman had too much make-up on. But her rounded cheeks, plump body, and even her hair pulled up into a tight bun reminded Mindy of her art teacher who was a kind woman. However, Mindy was horrified at the thought of telling her story to a stranger.

"No, ma'am. Thank you m'am. I'm quite all right." The woman continued to peer into Mindy's face. It was obvious that she didn't want to leave the frail girl alone. Mindy saw the look of concern and flashed the woman a smile that she hoped looked confident.

"My dad will be right here."

"Well, child, if he doesn't come, look me up. I work at Mademoiselle's." The woman pointed her gloved hand to a large purple building with green and pink awnings across the street and down the block. "My name is Harriet, and I can stop work any time to help a young friend."

"Thank you, Ma'am. But my father will be here. I just got here too early." Mindy hoped she sounded more confident than she felt.

Harriet walked away briskly, turning every so often to send a worried smile back at Mindy. Mindy tried to look perky. She remembered her grandmother saying, "Look perky, child. You wear your troubles on your sleeve — an open book for all the world to see." She tried not to look lost and hopeless, which was how she felt. She desperately hoped no one else would ask her what she was doing on this corner.

The fact was that Mindy wasn't early. No matter how much her adored father tried, he could never get to a place on time. Knowing her father, she had planned to be at this meeting place exactly on time. She knew he would be late, so she didn't want to be early. She also didn't want to be late and give him time to wander off window shopping in one of his daydreams. She had climbed into the taxi, given the man the address, and landed on the corner of Elm and Vine exactly at two o'clock.

The old church across from where Mindy stood had probably once seemed huge to the bypasser. Now it was dwarfed by the larger buildings around it. Still, it was an impressive place. The paved paths through its neat gardens, the lovely fountain, and the solid steps leading up to the great double wooden doors gave the church a look of commanding calm. It looked like a place where a person could go and be soothed. Mindy wished she could go now and sit by the fountain, but if she did that, her father surely would never find her. She looked at the large clock on the church tower.

Continued on page 66.

Two thirty! Even her absent minded father wouldn't have her stay in an unknown spot of this busy city for a half hour all by herself. She shivered in the coat she had chosen to wear. Her prettier coat wasn't nearly as warm as the dull practical one that she had left hanging in the closet. The thin, lacy dress beneath it wasn't much help either. She was starting to get cold, really cold, and scared. She stopped caring if she wore her emotions on her sleeve. She was scared, cold, alone, and angry with her father who had deserted her in this place filled with a thousand strangers.

"Listen, honey," a voice broke into her angry thoughts. She jumped and turned nervously to the loud voice. It was Harriet again. "I've been watching you from the shop. I don't understand what a little girl would be doing standing all alone on a street corner in this city. Come on in here. You can have a hot chocolate and tell me about it."

Mindy was about to refuse, but she couldn't think of any good reason to give. She let herself be led into the warm coffee shop.

"Where do you think you are going with my little girl?" boomed a deep voice behind them. Mindy was flooded with relief. Her father had come after all! She quickly untangled her hand from Harriet's gloved fingers and jumped into her father's open arms.

MAKING THE PICTURES WORK FOR YOU: REMEMBERING DETAILS

When you answered the questions about Mindy's story, you were probably using pictures in your mind or imagery. Imagining characters and scenes helps to make a story interesting. None of the answers were really in the story! You made them up in your mind's eye, that is, your imagination. When you get a picture of characters or scenery from reading or listening to a story, it shows that you have a creative imagination.

You can use this ability to *see in your mind's eye* to help you make sense of some details that may not be clear to you.

When you do the next exercise, you can put this imagination to work for you.

EXERCISE II

Directions: Your teacher will read a selection aloud called "The Body's Defense Against Disease." As you listen, try to picture the following things:

1.   The first line of defense is described as an obstacle course. Try to picture the obstacles that get in the way of germs.

2.   Part of the second line of defense is the white blood cells. Try to picture what the white blood cells look like as they surround a germ.

3.   The third line of defense is antibodies. When you hear about antibodies, try to form a picture of them.

4.   As you hear about the following things, try to get a picture of each one in your mind's eye: germs, lymph, capillaries, and infection.

When the reading is completed, you will be asked to answer some factual questions.

Again, it might help you to close your eyes, so you can picture things without interference as you listen.

ANSWER THESE QUESTIONS

1. Name two things that provide an obstacle course in the body's first line of defense.

    _____

    _____

2. How do white blood cells help the body protect you from germs? _____

    _____

    _____

3. What is a capillary? _____

4. What does an antibody do to protect you from germs? _____

    _____

    _____

5. How does lymph help your body to handle germs? _____

    _____

    _____

FOR FUN

1. Draw a germ as you pictured it.

2. Did any other interesting visual images come into your mind as you listened? If so, draw or explain them in words.

KINDS OF PICTURES IN YOUR MIND'S EYE

When people imagine, they often see pictures or images in their mind's eye. Sometimes the imagination includes other senses as well: hearing, smelling, touching, even tasting. In fact, when some people imagine, they don't see pictures at all. Instead they hear, smell, touch, taste, or all of these.

Everyone can imagine, but we all use our imagination in our own personal way. What do you experience when *you* imagine?

SOLVE YOUR PROBLEMS BY PICTURING THE STEPS

Sometimes you have an idea for a project you want to do. You can picture, or see in your mind's eye, a completed task. For example, you can imagine the tent when it is set up. You can imagine how the paper mache model will turn out. You can imagine how you want your salt and flour map to look, and so on.

However, when you start to work on the project, you find that the picture in your mind isn't as helpful as you had hoped. You don't know how to begin.

In the unit *A Matter of Time,* you had to plan steps so you could reach your goal. When you are doing a project like the ones described above, writing down the steps often isn't enough. You have to be able to picture what each step will look like when it is completed. The next exercise shows you a way that you can do this.

EXERCISE III

Directions: Below you'll find three methods for making a paper airplane. Try out each method, and discover which one works best for you. Use imagery to picture each step as you go.

METHOD I

Study the picture below. Then take one of the sheets that your teacher gave you. Try to construct the paper airplane pictured.

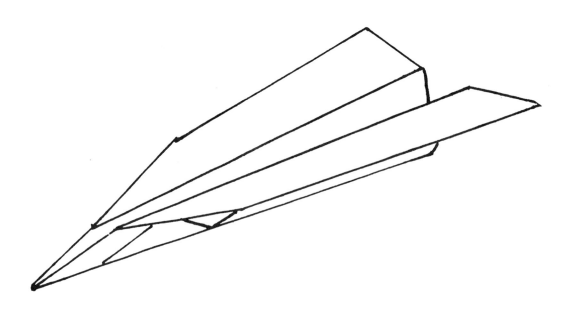

METHOD II

Read the step-by-step instructions below. Follow each of the steps. Try to construct the paper airplane they describe.

STEP 1

Use a sheet of 8½″ x 11″ paper. Crease-fold the paper in half first. Then open it. Fold the top corners down.

STEP 2

Hold the paper lengthwise. Call the top left point A and the bottom left point B. Fold A and B down about a quarter of the sides to the crease. Make sure A and B touch on the center crease.

STEP 3

Call the top points of the airplane's nose C and D. Fold in points C and D. The top two edges should meet each other on the center crease.

STEP 4

Fold the entire airplane in half in the opposite direction.

STEP 5

Fold the wings down to meet the bottom edge of the fuselage.

STEP 6

Curl the tail section up slightly for better lift.

METHOD III

Look at the pictures in the steps below. The pictures show what the airplane should look like *as* you follow the directions for each step. Try to match what you are doing to what you see.

STEP 1

Use a sheet of 8½″ x 11″ paper. Crease-fold the paper in half first. Then open it. Fold the top corners down.

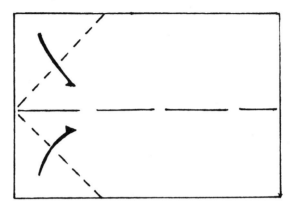

STEP 2

Fold in the sides. Make sure that points A and B touch each other on the center crease.

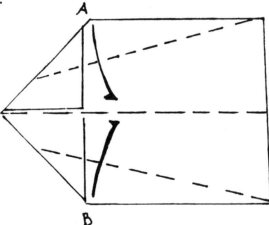

STEP 3

Fold in points C and D. The top two edges should meet each other on the center crease.

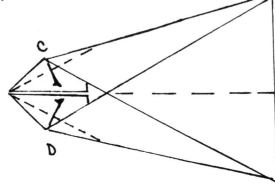

STEP 4

Fold the entire airplane in half in the opposite direction.

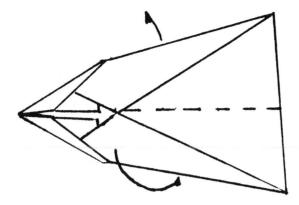

STEP 5

Fold the wings down to meet the bottom edge of the fuselage.

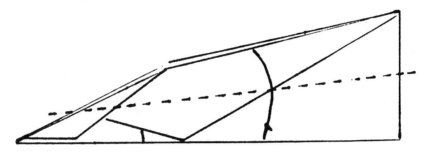

STEP 6

Curl the tail section up slightly for better lift.

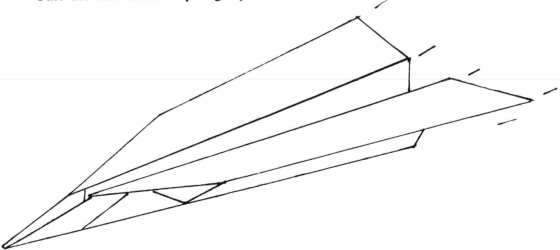

EXERCISE IV

Directions: Look at the map below. You have to copy this map in the space below it as accurately as possible. Can you think of a way to break this task into steps? Discuss this problem with your classmates and teacher before you begin.

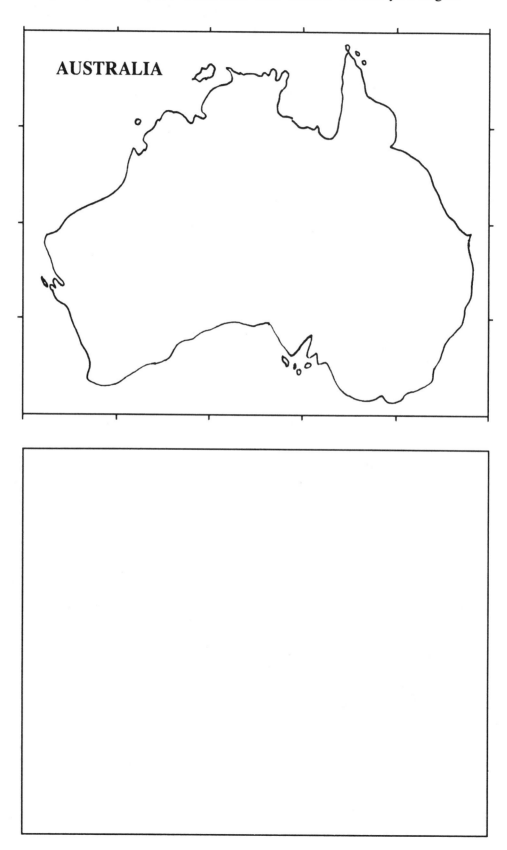

AUSTRALIA

UNIT VI SUMMARY: PICTURING IN YOUR MIND'S EYE

Most people have the ability to imagine or see pictures in their mind's eye. Sometimes the imagination uses your other senses: hearing, smelling, feeling, even tasting.

These pictures or images can help to make reading and hearing stories more interesting to you. You can also remember important details when you form images of them.

The ability to picture things in your mind's eye is often helpful in solving problems. When you use your imagination to help you solve a problem, break the problem down into small, easy-to-do steps. Then do one step at a time.

UNIT VII: READING FOR MEANING

HOW DO YOU READ?

*"Read the assignment in your book,
and be ready for a quiz!"*

This is a direction you probably often hear in school. When you are given this direction, what do you do?

Look at the reading on page 77 of this unit. If your teacher asked you to read this and be ready for a quiz about it, what would you do? On the lines below, briefly describe *how* you would complete this assignment.

REMEMBER: Don't actually read the section now. Just describe *how* you would read it.

_____

_____

_____

_____

_____

_____

THE RACE TO THE MOON

Sputnik launched!

On October 4, 1957, the U.S.S.R. astounded the American public by launching Sputnik I. Sputnik I was the first man-made satellite to orbit the earth. On November 3rd of the same year, the Soviets sent another Sputnik, Sputnik II, into orbit, carrying a dog named Laika. The race to the moon was on.

The United States responds.

The United States was caught off guard by the advanced technology of the Soviet space program. In the year following the launching of Sputnik I, the United States Congress authorized billions of dollars to be put into an American space program. NASA, the National Aeronautics and Space Administration, was created in 1958. In that same year the United States launched its first satellite, Explorer I.

The first travelers in space

A few years later the Soviet Union sent the first traveler into outer space. On April 7, 1961, Yuri Gagarin became the first man to journey into the farthest reaches of the Earth's atmosphere. In 1963 Valentina Tereshkova became the first woman to fly into outer space.

The first American astronaut

In the years between 1961 and 1963 the American space program was also busy. The United States launched its first manned flight in May 1961. Alan Shepherd rode a tiny capsule which was launched from Cape Canaveral in Florida. Shepherd's flight lasted only fifteen minutes. Americans huddled around their TV sets to watch the launch. Telstar, the first communications satellite, was also launched in 1961.

Amazing breakthroughs in 1965

Amazing breakthroughs engineered by both countries took place in 1965. Leonov of the U.S.S.R. made the first space walk from the Voshkod spacecraft. The United States launched the first of the Gemini space flights, each of which orbited the Earth many times. Luna 9 of the U.S.S.R. and Surveyor I of the U.S.A. were both unmanned spacecrafts which made soft landings on the moon during this year. A Soviet probe crash-landed on Venus. And the U.S.'s Mariner 4 transmitted the first close-up pictures of Mars over a distance of 217 million kilometers.

Orbiting the moon

After many different kinds of space experiments had been conducted by both nations, the United States made a great thrust to the moon in 1968. The American astronauts Frank Borman, William Anders, and James Lovell, Jr. orbited the moon ten times on December 24-25 of that year.

Moon landing!

Finally in July 1969 American astronauts Armstrong and Aldrin placed their feet on the surface of the moon. The race between nations was over. The plaque the astronauts left on the moon said: "Here men from Earth first set forth on the moon. July 1969 A.D. We came in peace for all mankind."

INTRODUCTION

You've probably discovered that many students don't have a special way of reading a textbook. What they usually do is start with the first word in the assignment and read as far as they get. Unfortunately this isn't a very good way to learn from your reading.

This unit will show you a way of reading an assignment in a textbook and learning from your reading. This method is called READING FOR MEANING. You may find that this method is new to you and will take a little more time at first. You might also find it a little tricky. Stay with it! Learn how to use this method, and you will become a better learner.

READING FOR MEANING

When you read a paragraph or section in your textbook, what you really want to find out is:

What is the *main idea* of this reading?

What are the *important details* that support the *main idea?*

READING FOR MEANING means locating *main ideas* and the *supporting details* in your reading.

Another way to think of READING FOR MEANING is this: when you read for meaning, you're trying to find out what the paragraph or section is trying to tell you. Ask yourself these questions:

What does the person who wrote this paragraph or section want me to know?

What is this paragraph or section trying to tell me?

EXERCISE I

Directions: Read the paragraph below. Then write the main idea of the paragraph on the lines that follow.

REMEMBER: The *main idea* in a paragraph is the most important idea. It is the idea that the rest of the paragraph is about.

The *main idea* is the idea that the writer is trying to share with you.

PARAGRAPH A

Dogs have a very powerful sense of smell that they can use to find things. Police use tracking dogs to search for people who are missing in the woods. The dogs sniff a piece of clothing owned by the missing person. Then they try to track the scent in the area where the person was last seen. Often these dogs can find people who are lost when the police have no other way of locating them. Another kind of tracking dog is the hunting hound. These dogs can follow animals for miles through the forest once they have sniffed their scent. Though some dogs are better than others in using their sense of smell, all dogs have a stronger sense of smell than people do.

_____

_____

MAIN IDEA AND SUPPORTING DETAILS

We know that the *main idea* of a paragraph is the most important idea in that paragraph. It's the idea that the rest of the paragraph is about.

Most paragraphs also have *supporting details*. Supporting details explain, prove, or tell something about the main idea of the paragraph. They make the main idea more clear to us or give us more information about it.

These details are called *"supporting"* details because they *"hold up"* the main idea. This means that they give us reasons to believe the main idea and help us to understand it.

EXERCISE II

Directions: Read the paragraph on page 79 again. On the lines below, list *two* supporting details for the main idea.

PARAGRAPH A

1. _____

2. _____

EXERCISE III

Directions: Find the main idea for the paragraph below. Then locate two supporting details. Write the main idea and supporting details on the appropriate lines. Do the same for Paragraphs C and D on page 82.

PARAGRAPH B

In the early days America was a country full of individuals who did many things well. One man stands out from all the rest. This man helped to organize many institutions in the new country: the United States Post Office; the Pennsylvania Academy; Pennsylvania Hospital, the first in America. He also organized the first American expedition to the Arctic region. He was an inventor, inventing many useful things including the Franklin stove, the lightning rod, bifocal glasses, and an instrument he call the "armonica." He also wrote books and newspapers and took part in the politics of early America. Benjamin Franklin was a man of many talents.

Main Idea: _____

_____

Supporting details:

1. _____

2. _____

PARAGRAPH C

She was an adult female who died three million years ago. The archaeologists who found her bones nicknamed her "Lucy." They did not find her entire skeleton. However, a description of Lucy can be based on the bones they found. She was a Hominidae, a primate that stood and walked on two legs. She had a skeleton much like ours. But she was tiny compared to today's humans. She stood three feet, eight inches tall and weighed about 65 pounds. Her thick bones show that she must have had great muscular strength. Lucy's face and apelike jutting jaws were large, but her brain was probably only one third the size of a modern human's.

Main Idea: _____

_____

Supporting details:

1. _____

2. _____

PARAGRAPH D

The man lowered a hydrophone into the water. This phone was meant to pick up the clicks, whistles, and short piercing screams of the killer whales. He explained that the clicks seem to be a way that the whales tell each other where food is located. The whistles are heard most often between resting or socializing whales. But, he explained, the most interesting of all are the screams. They are different within each whale pod (a pod is a group of whales). This suggests that whales are among the few animals that have a local dialect or a special way of speaking to the others that live in the same region.

Main Idea: _____

_____

Supporting details:

1. _____

2. _____

HOW DO YOU FIND THE MAIN IDEA?

The main idea of a paragraph is stated in the *topic sentence*. The purpose of the *topic sentence* is to tell you the main idea. For example, in the paragraph about the strong sense of smell that dogs have, the topic sentence is the first one.

When you read a paragraph, the main idea will sometimes be very clear to you. When it's not clear, use these hints for finding it:

1. Most often the topic sentence is the first sentence in the paragraph. This means that you'll often find the main idea in the first sentence of a paragraph.

2. Sometimes the topic sentence is the last sentence in a paragraph. When the first sentence doesn't tell you the main idea, look at the last sentence in the paragraph and see if it's there.

3. In some paragraphs, the topic sentence is in the middle of the paragraph. In these paragraphs, you can only find the main idea by reading the paragraph carefully and figuring out what the paragraph is telling you.

4. In some paragraphs, there is no topic sentence. The main idea is not stated clearly in any one sentence of the paragraph. Often this happens when the main idea has already been stated in another paragraph. When this happens, you really have to read carefully to see if you can figure out what the paragraph is trying to tell you.

HOW TO READ FOR MEANING

Reading for meaning means finding the main idea and supporting details in your reading. You can read for meaning by using these four steps:

SURVEYING
READING
MAPPING
CHECKING YOURSELF

STEP #1: SURVEYING

When you first start to read a paragraph, don't read it word for word. Instead *SURVEY* the paragraph first.

SURVEYING means to look quickly at any heading or titles over the paragraph and then read the first and last sentences. *SURVEYING* will usually let you find out what the paragraph is about. And it takes only a minute or less!

EXERCISE IV

Directions: *SURVEY* the paragraph below. On the lines below it, write what you think the *main idea* of this paragraph is.

A PROFIT IN FROGS

People don't usually think of frog raising as a profitable business, but many people are willing to pay for frogs. Universities and high schools buy frogs for use in their science labs. Restaurants will pay $4.50 or more for a pound of dressed frog meat, as frogs are considered a delicacy by many people. NASA uses frogs in space and will pay $25 or more for a healthy bullfrog. Probably more frogs have orbited the earth than people. People who own ponds will also buy frogs because frogs can help to keep down the insect population. So, the next time that you think about leaving a frog in your teacher's desk, you may decide that there's a more profitable use for your hopping, green friend.

_____

_____

STEP #2: READING

Once you've *SURVEYED* a paragraph, you usually have a sense of what the *main idea* is. Now *READ* the paragraph at your normal rate of reading. As you *READ,* look for SUPPORTING DETAILS that prove, explain, or tell you more about the main idea.

EXERCISE V

Directions: Read the paragraph about "A Profit In Frogs." As you read, be sure to look for supporting details. List at least two details on the lines below.

_____

_____

STEP #3: MAPPING

MAPPING is a way of taking notes about your reading. Look at the *MAP* below for the paragraph about frogs.

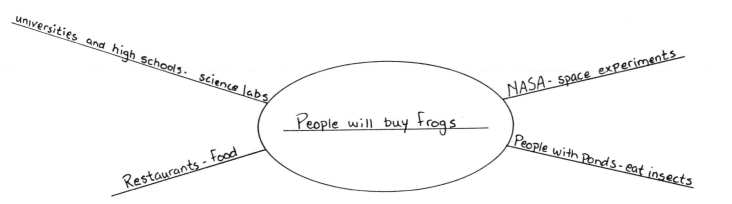

You can take *MAPPING* notes in this way:

1. First write the MAIN IDEA on a line in the middle of your paper. Then circle the MAIN IDEA.

2. List each SUPPORTING DETAIL that you find on a line that touches the circle around the MAIN IDEA.

MAPPING is a way of taking notes that helps you to understand what the main idea is and what the supporting details are.

EXERCISE VI

Directions: Survey the paragraph below. Then read it and take notes in the *MAP* below the paragraph.

SMART CHIMPS!

Chimpanzees are among the most intelligent animals on earth other than human beings. The structure or makeup of the chimpanzee brain is a lot like the structure of the human brain. Chimps have the ability to use simple tools. In recent years, scientists have found that chimps communicate with each other through noises and gestures. Chimps also seem to be able to learn words and make signs that stand for words.

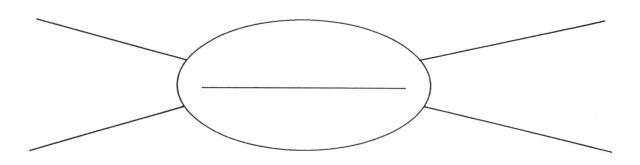

STEP #4: CHECKING YOURSELF

Now, look at your mapping notes and *CHECK YOURSELF*. Using only your notes, tell yourself what the reading is about. Or tell someone who hasn't read the paragraph.

When you take a little time to CHECK YOURSELF, you'll see what you have learned. And you'll find it much easier to remember what you have read.

EXERCISE VII

Directions: Go back and look through the four steps. They are these:

> SURVEYING
> READING
> MAPPING
> CHECKING YOURSELF

Then use the four steps to *read for meaning* the three paragraphs on this page and the next.

VISITORS FROM OUTER SPACE

You may not believe in extra-terrestrial life forms, but the fact is that we get "visitors" from outer space daily. Each year at least 20,000 tons of material from meteors enters our atmosphere. This means about 50 tons a day! Chances of the meteors being big enough to cause us any harm are incredibly slim. The earth's atmosphere burns up the material from outer space before it can reach the surface of the earth. Only 10 to 20 new meteors are actually found on the earth's surface each year. But as they enter the earth's atmosphere, the burning can be seen from earth as a streak of light. So, we should be able to locate "a falling star" on any clear night.

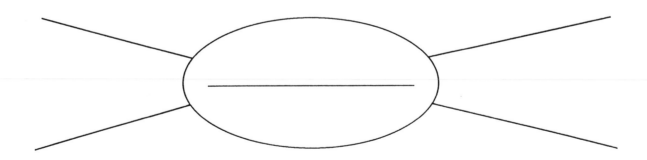

THE WORLD HAS BEEN ROUND FOR A LONG TIME!

Some say that Columbus discovered that the world was round. This is not entirely true. Many people knew the world was round long before the days of Columbus. The Greek mathematician, Pythagoras, declared that the world was round in the sixth century B.C. Hundreds of years before the birth of Christ, Eratosthenes figured the distance around the world. During the same time period, Aristotle reported rumors of lands on the other side of the globe. The Greek map maker, Strabo, wrote of men's attempts to sail around the world in the 7th century A.D. Many well educated men of Columbus's day agreed with Columbus that it was perfectly possible to reach the east by sailing west because the earth was a sphere. So, you see, the idea that the earth is round has been around for a long time.

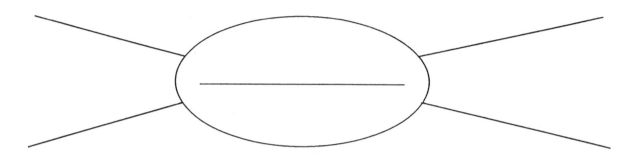

THE GENTLE APE

It's hard to imagine any relative of King Kong as being gentle. But according to Dr. Francine Paterson, the 230 pound Koko is just that. Koko is a lowland female gorilla who has been working with Dr. Paterson for over a decade. By the use of sign language, Koko let Dr. Paterson know that she wanted a kitten for her birthday. When Paterson gave her a little kitten, Koko was delighted. She spent many hours playing with the tiny animal, carrying her kitten from place to place, gently stroking its fur, and bending over to give it a kiss. When the kitten died, Koko was struck with deep grief. It wasn't until the kitten was replaced that Koko resumed her normal activities. It might also interest you to know that Koko is a vegetarian. She obviously prefers petting small creatures to eating them!

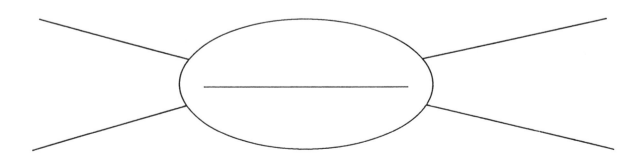

WHY TAKE NOTES?

"Taking notes is a lot of work. Why bother?"

Have you ever said this? Or heard a friend say it? Well, why should you take notes? Here are two good reasons for taking notes:

1. When you take notes, you learn by writing the main idea and supporting details down on your paper. You'll understand your reading better if you take a few minutes to write down your notes. You'll also remember the main idea and supporting details better.

2. When you take notes, you have a record of what you've read. You can use the record to study for tests.

UNIT VII SUMMARY: READING FOR MEANING

READING FOR MEANING means locating *main ideas* and the important *supporting details* in your reading.

The *main idea* in a paragraph is the most important idea. It is the idea that the rest of the paragraph is about.

Supporting details explain, prove, or tell something more about the main idea. They make the main idea more clear or give more information about it.

The main idea of a paragraph is often stated in the *topic sentence*. Most often the topic sentence is the first sentence in the paragraph. It can also be the last sentence or in the middle of the paragraph.

How do you READ FOR MEANING? Use these four steps:

1. SURVEYING: Look quickly at any headings or titles above the paragraph. Then read the first and last sentences of the paragraph. SURVEYING will usually help you find out what the *main idea* is.

2. READING: Read the paragraph at your normal rate of reading. As you read, look for *supporting details*.

3. MAPPING: Make a map like the one below to take notes from your reading. MAPPING helps you to learn the *main idea* and *supporting details* of the reading. It also gives you a record of the reading that you can use later.

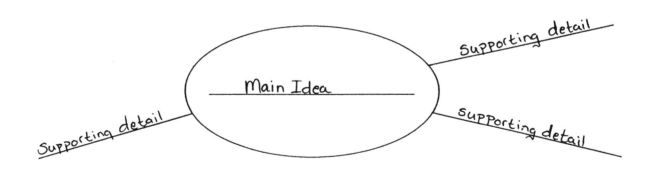

4. CHECKING YOURSELF: Look at your MAPPING notes and tell yourself what the reading is about. Or ask yourself: what have I learned from reading this?

UNIT VIII: TAKING NOTES — MAPPING AND OUTLINING

INTRODUCTION

In the unit about READING FOR MEANING, you learned about *mapping* as a way of taking notes. This unit will help you to learn more about how to use *mapping*. It will also help you to learn about another way of taking notes called *outlining*.

> **REMEMBER:** Taking notes helps you to learn more about what you are reading or hearing. Also, when you take notes, you have a record to study when you have a test.

TIPS FOR TAKING NOTES

1. Your notes are for you! Take notes that make sense to you. This means that you can use words from your reading, too, but be sure you understand what your notes say.

2. When you take notes, you don't need to write in complete sentences. Write down only the words and phrases that tell you the main ideas and important details in your reading. You can also use abbreviations and symbols.

3. Don't write down everything in your reading. Write down only the main ideas and important details in your notes.

BREAKING DOWN SENTENCES

When you take notes, you want to write as few words as possible that tell the important ideas and information. One way to do this is *breaking down* the sentences in your reading into a few key words.

Look at the sentence below:

In 1977 *Star Wars,* a movie that was directed by George Lucas, who had graduated from a California film school only a few years earlier, began to play in theaters all over the country with great success.

Now, look at an example of the notes from this sentence:

1977 — *Star Wars* — great success — by George Lucas.

When you break down a sentence, try to write as few words as you can. But be sure to keep the important ideas and information.

EXERCISE I

Directions: Read the sentences below. *Break down* each into as few words as possible that tell the important ideas and information.

1. The stories of Greek myths make good reading, for the gods and goddesses are dramatically filled with human emotion: love, hate, and jealousy.

   _____

2. Energy that was created from wind power could save the states of the windy north from their need to burn fuel.

   _____

3. The apple, the delicious fruit of the Garden of Eden, is an important fall harvest for the state of New York.

   _____

4. In the late eighteen forties many people made a mad dash to California hoping to get rich through the discovery of gold.

   _____

5. The fair-haired, tall, and hard fighting sailor of Scandinavia was known as the Viking.

   _____

EXERCISE II

Directions: Read the paragraph below using the four steps you learned in the last unit. Do you remember them?

SURVEYING
READING
MAPPING
CHECKING YOURSELF

Also use the *Tips for Taking Notes* that you read on page 91 in this unit.

Sioux Indian children were taught to swim at a very early age. When the baby was two months old, its mother would take it to a quiet spot along the river bank. She would place her hands gently under the baby's belly and place him or her into the shallow, warm water until it came up around him or her. Then suddenly the baby's sturdy legs would begin to kick and his or her arms to whip through the water. The next time the baby lasted a little longer, and by the third or fourth time the mother could take her hands away for a bit while the baby held his or her head up and dogpaddled for himself or herself.

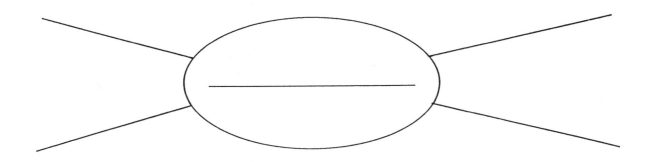

ANOTHER WAY TO TAKE NOTES: MAPPING WITH NUMBERS

You may have had some difficulty in drawing up your MAP for the paragraph about the Sioux baby. Maybe you asked yourself questions like these:

How do I know which line I should start with?

Can any detail go on any line? Or is there a place where each one belongs?

When the reading about which you are taking notes is organized in a certain order or sequence, you can still use a kind of MAPPING for your note taking. You do this by numbering the *supporting details* on your MAP. The details show the order of the sequence.

Look at the map below, and you'll see an example of MAPPING WITH NUMBERS.

SIOUX BABIES TAUGHT TO SWIM

1. Two months old - mother takes baby to river

2. Places her hands under baby's belly

3. Puts into shallow, warm water

4. Legs begin to kick - arms whip through water

EXERCISE III

Directions: Try to map the paragraph below by MAPPING WITH NUMBERS.

In its short lifetime, the butterfly goes through four complete changes. We can call these changes "Stages of Life for the Butterfly." The first stage is the egg stage. The adult female chooses a good food source to lay her eggs on. The second stage is the larvae or caterpillar stage. When the eggs hatch, the hungry caterpillars soon devour the leaves around them. They need to eat a lot because they don't eat at all in their third stage, and many don't eat in the fourth stage. Their third stage is spent resting in a cocoon or pupa chrysalis. Finally the adult emerges from the cocoon. In the last stage of life, the butterfly's main job is to mate and lay eggs.

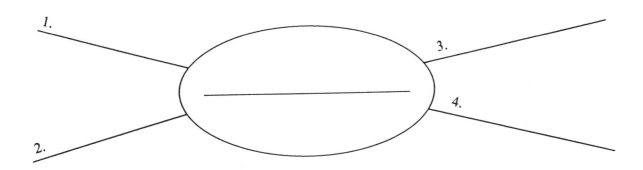

A THIRD WAY TO TAKE NOTES: OUTLINING

When a paragraph is organized into a certain sequence of events, it is easy to use a third way of taking notes called OUTLINING. This is much the same as MAPPING WITH NUMBERS, but the way the information is set up is different.

Look below, and you'll see the form for OUTLINING.

OUTLINE FORM

I. Main Idea

    A. Supporting detail

    B. Supporting detail

    C. Supporting detail

HOW TO OUTLINE

1. Use a Roman numeral to list main ideas.

2. Use capital letters to list supporting details. Indent each capital letter a little way to the right of the Roman numeral.

EXERCISE IV

Directions: Write your notes about the butterfly in the outine form below.

I. _____

    A. _____

    B. _____

    C. _____

    D. _____

EXERCISE V

Directions: Read the paragraph below, and take notes for it on the outline form below.

What causes hail? If you've ever had to run for cover to escape from the pounding of a hailstorm in the middle of what had been a hot and sticky day in July, you've probably asked yourself the same question. It usually hails in hot weather just before a violent thunderstorm. First cold air gets pushed up above the heavy, warm air. This causes strong upward winds. As it begins to rain, the raindrops are blown upward by these winds. The rain freezes in the cold upper air before it falls to the earth. Each time the droplets fall through the warm air, they gather more moisture. Each time the larger droplets are blow into the cold upper air, they freeze into larger ice balls. When this cycle repeats itself several times, you'll see hail that is the size of golf balls. So hail is created when the raindrops are blown into the colder air over and over again, causing them to freeze into hailstones.

I. _____

    A. _____

    B. _____

    C. _____

    D. _____

    E. _____

HOW SHOULD *YOU* TAKE NOTES?

You have tried out three different ways of taking notes in this unit: mapping, mapping with numbers, and outlining. All three of these methods can be helpful to you.

Use a way of taking notes that makes sense to you. Experiment with these three ways of taking notes until you find the way that best fits the way that you learn.

You may want to use different note taking methods at different times. Look carefully at the kind of reading that you're taking notes about. Then decide which way of taking notes will work best for you.

    REMEMBER: Your notes are for you! Take notes in your own words that make sense to you.

UNIT VIII SUMMARY: TAKING NOTES—MAPPING AND OUTLINING

Three good ways of taking notes are: OUTLINING
MAPPING
MAPPING WITH NUMBERS

OUTLINING

I. Main Idea

    A. Supporting detail
    B. Supporting detail
    C. Supporting detail
    D. Supporting detail

MAPPING

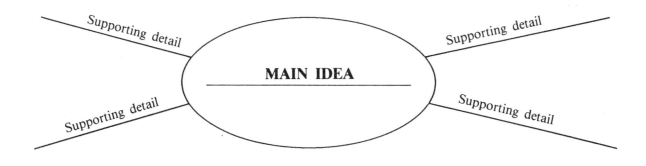

MAPPING WITH NUMBERS

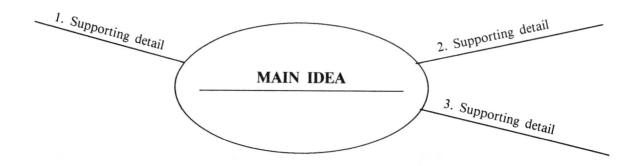

UNIT IX: LISTENING AND TAKING NOTES

INTRODUCTION

In the previous two units, you learned about three ways of taking notes:

outling
mapping
mapping with numbers

You have already used two of these note taking methods to take notes from reading. These methods can be useful to you in many other ways. One of these ways is taking notes from listening.

This unit will give you practice in listening and taking notes.

LISTENING AND TAKING NOTES

Much of what you need to learn to do well in any class will be covered in the class itself. One way to learn more in class is to take notes.

Taking *brief* notes in class can help you learn in the following ways:

1. Taking notes in class can help you to find the main ideas of what is being said, because you'll only want to write down the main ideas.

2. Writing down the main ideas as notes will help you to learn them better.

3. When you take notes in class, you can use your notes later to study for a test.

HOW DO YOU START?

Before you start to take notes from listening, decide which note taking method best fits your way of learning. At first, use the method with which you are most comfortable, the one that seems the easiest for you.

Once you feel comfortable with one note taking method, try using others. You may want to follow these suggestions:

1. You can use the *outline* method for any kind of organized talk. In an organized talk, the speaker has put the main ideas and important details into an order to share with you. Sometimes your teacher will put an *outline* on the board at the beginning of class or during class. Use this *outline* as a starting point for your *outline* notes.

2. You can also use the *mapping with numbers* method for an organized talk.

3. You can use the *mapping* method or the *mapping with numbers* method for taking notes during any activity that is less organized, such as a class discussion or question period.

TIPS FOR TAKING NOTES FROM LISTENING

1. Be an *active* listener! Try to make sense of what the speaker is saying. Try to connect what the speaker is saying with what you already know.

2. If you can, "picture" in your mind what is being said.

3. Before you start to take notes, think about how the speaker has organized what he or she will say. For example, is there an outline on the board? Is it a class discussion? Then decide what method you want to use to take notes.

4. Try to spend most of your time listening. Figure out what the main ideas are, and write them down. Use only words and phrases, not complete sentences. Remember: your notes are for you; make sure they make sense to you!

5. When your teacher tells you that you'll need to know something, be sure to write it down.

EXERCISE I

Directions: Your teacher will give a talk for a few minutes. Take notes from the talk in the space below.

LOOKING AT YOUR NOTES

Directions: Look carefully at your notes from Exercise I. Then answer the questions below.

1. What note taking method did you use? _____

    _____

2. How well did this method work for you? _____

    _____

    _____

3. Do your notes make sense to you? _____

    _____

4. How could you make your notes better or more helpful to you? _____

    _____

    _____

EXERCISE II

Directions: Your teacher will lead a short class discussion. Take notes from the discussion in the space below.

LOOKING AGAIN AT YOUR NOTES

Directions: Look carefully at your notes from Exercise II. Then answer the questions below.

1. Did you use the same note taking method that you used for Exercise I?

    _____

2. Explain why you chose the method that you used. _____

    _____

    _____

    _____

3. How is taking notes during a class discussion different from taking notes during a lecture?

    _____

    _____

4. Do your notes make sense to you? _____

5. How could you make your notes better or more helpful to you?

    _____

    _____

UNIT IX SUMMARY: LISTENING AND TAKING NOTES

Much of what you need to learn for any class will be covered in the class itself. Taking *brief* notes in class can help you with this learning.

Use a note taking method with which you are comfortable when you start. Later on, you may want to use different methods in different situations. For example:

1. You can use the *outline* method for any kind of organized talk. You can also use *mapping with numbers* for an organized talk.

2. You can use the *mapping* method or *mapping with numbers* for taking notes during a less organized activity, such as a class discussion.

Be an *active* listener! Try to make sense of what the speaker is saying. Spend most of your time listening. Figure out what the main ideas are, and write them down in words and phrases.

REMEMBER: Your notes are for you. Take notes that make sense to you.

UNIT X: IMPROVING YOUR VOCABULARY

INTRODUCTION

Your vocabulary includes all of the words that you can understand and use in your thinking, speaking, writing, and reading.

Did you know that the average elementary school student increases his or her vocabulary by about 1000 words every year? The average junior high or middle school student increases his or her vocabulary by almost 2000 words each year!

One important way that you learn new words is through your reading. However, when you are reading, there are some problems that you may have in learning about unknown or unfamiliar words.

1. By now, you probably can read quickly enough so that you may skip over words without realizing that you don't understand them.

2. To look up a word in the dictionary, you have to stop reading. This interrupts the flow of your reading.

3. When you use a dictionary, you must be able to choose the correct meaning from all the meanings listed.

This unit and Unit XIII will help you to learn ways to solve these problems.

EXERCISE I

Directions: Your teacher will read the three paragraphs below to you. Pay careful attention to the underlined words. Think about the meaning of these words. When your teacher has finished reading, write the definitions of the underlined words on the lines below.

I wish they hadn't been so worried about us. Jeannie and I had only taken the canoe for a quick trip down the lake.

The day had been a breezy and blue one with lots of sunshine. The sunlight gleamed off the *ridges* of the waves. We tried at first to paddle, but the wind was so strong that it controlled our course. Since our paddling was useless, we *eased* ourselves down and rested against the cushions. We didn't know that sitting on the floor of the canoe was the best thing to do to keep the canoe *upright*.

As the wind grew stronger and the waves rose higher, the canoe began to rise and fall. We would be about to topple over the *crest* of a wave when our well-*dispersed* weight would balance us. Then we would slide easily down the watery slope. *Peering* over the boat's edge was like looking down from a roller coaster. We were rising and falling with each huge, rolling wave.

ridges _____

eased _____

upright _____

crest _____

dispersed _____

peering _____

LEARNING ABOUT NEW WORDS

When you come across an unknown or unfamiliar word in your reading, you can learn its meaning in two ways.

1. You can look up the word in the dictionary.

2. You can often figure out the meaning of a new word by looking carefully at the meaning of the words and phrases around it. This is called getting the meaning from *CONTEXT CLUES*. Some of you may have used this method in Exercise I.

   A *context* is the setting in which something is found. For example, a museum is a context in which paintings are displayed. A gym is a context in which people play basketball. You expect to find certain things because of the context.

   In language, *context* means the words and sentences around any particular word. *CONTEXT CLUES* are familiar words and phrases in a sentence or paragraph. These are words that you know. From these familiar words, you can often figure out the meaning of an unknown word.

EXAMPLE   Many animals are *extinct*, such as dinosaurs.

extinct means _____

EXERCISE II

Directions: Read the rest of the story about the canoeing adventure below. When you find a word that stops you because you are not sure of its meaning, underline the word.

I didn't worry. Jeannie and I were both strong swimmers. The shore wasn't very far away if the canoe decided to turn us into the foaming waters. I daydreamed that we were sailors on the ocean, conquerors of the deep. Poseidon, with all his power, could not entice us to his kingdom.

The ride finally stopped on the southwest side of the vast lake. The canoe came to a natural halt where the waters lapped gently against a small island. Suddenly we realized that we could never paddle back against those waves.

We would have to wait. The lake would become still towards evening. Jeannie and I climbed out of the canoe and found a healthy patch of blueberries. While we devoured the blueberries, we felt completely carefree. Neither of us realized that we were in big trouble.

Then I spied my uncle. He came in a motor boat. The boat slapped against the waves and sprayed water high into the air. He had come looking for us, probably half expecting the canoe to be capsized with two victims floating face down beside it. I knew he was relieved that we were alive. I also knew that his relief would soon turn to anger because we had been so foolish and had caused everyone at home to worry. I stood staring at my toes and felt the exhilaration of the day pour out of me.

EXERCISE III

Directions: On the lines for the new words below, write the words that you have underlined in the canoeing story. Then try to figure out the meaning of each word that you have listed from its *context clues*. Write your meaning in the space to the right of the word.

NEW WORDS   **MEANING**

_____   _____

                             _____

_____   _____

                             _____

_____   _____

                             _____

_____   _____

                             _____

_____   _____

                             _____

_____   _____

                             _____

_____   _____

                             _____

EXERCISE IV

Directions: Choose the best meaning for the numbered words below from the canoeing story. Mark an "X" on the line in front of the best meaning. Look at the word "vast" below as an example.

EXAMPLE

vast   a. _____ blue   c. _____ shallow
              b. _____ far   d. _x_ huge

✶✶✶✶✶✶✶✶✶✶✶✶✶✶✶✶✶✶✶✶✶✶✶✶✶✶✶✶✶✶✶✶✶✶✶✶✶

1. devouring   a. _____ eating   c. _____ smashing
               b. _____ throwing around   d. _____ eating hungrily

2. spied   a. _____ looked at   c. _____ spotted
               b. _____ looked secretly   d. _____ noticed

3. Poseidon   a. _____ a whale   c. _____ god of the sea in Greek
                                                         mythology
               b. _____ a king   d. _____ my uncle

4. capsized   a. _____ head size measure   c. _____ turned over
               b. _____ thrown down   d. _____ collapsed

5. victim   a. _____ someone who is hurt   c. _____ the target
                       or injured
               b. _____ the weaker one   d. _____ feeling sad

6. relieved   a. _____ replacement   c. _____ jump around
               b. _____ let go of worry   d. _____ feel a little better

7. exhilaration a. _____ feeling of   c. _____ smashing
                        disappointment
                b. _____ feeling of sadness   d. _____ feeling of great
                                                         excitement

8. conquerors a. _____ sailors   c. _____ great boats
               b. _____ ones who gain control d. _____ captains

112

HOW CAN YOU LEARN NEW WORDS FROM YOUR READING

1. Keep a special section in your notebook for new words. In this section, write down all the new words that you come across and their meanings.

2. When you come across a word from your reading that you don't fully understand, first try to figure out its meaning from *context clues.*

3. When you can't figure out the meaning of a new word from its *context clues,* you need to look it up in the dictionary to know what the word means.

UNIT X SUMMARY: IMPROVING YOUR VOCABULARY

A context is the setting in which something is found. In language, context means the words and the sentences around any particular word.

Context clues are familiar words and phrases in a sentence or paragraph. From these familiar words, you can often figure out the meaning of an unknown word.

When you come across a new word in your reading, first try to figure out its meaning from its context clues. If you can't, you need to look it up in the dictionary.

UNIT XI: ORGANIZING IDEAS

INTRODUCTION

In the unit *PUTTING IDEAS TOGETHER,* you saw how organizing ideas and information into categories can help your memory. This skill is useful in many other ways. For example, you can find your clothes in a drawer more easily if each drawer holds a certain *category* or type of clothes. You can find information in a school notebook more efficiently if there are *categories* or sections. You would even find cooking an easier task if like ingredients are stored in categories or on certain shelves in your kichen.

When you *organize ideas and information* into categories, the name of each category that you create is a *main idea.* Each idea or piece of information in the category is a *detail.*

In the shopping list below, the *main ideas* are at the top of each list of details.

EXAMPLE SITUATION:

You have to go shopping, and you only have a certain amount of time. You have to find the things on your list quickly. So you organize your list into the sections of the grocery store:

Dairy	Baking Goods	Produce	Frozen
milk	corn meal	oranges	ice cream
eggs	baking soda	celery	tv dinner
yogurt	chocolate chips	sprouts	frozen corn
butter	brown sugar	lettuce	
cheese	flour	carrots	
	baking powder	onions	
		radishes	
		spinach	
		apples	

EXERCISE I

Directions: Read the situations below and on page 116. Each situation requires you to make a list so that you can do the work more efficiently.

Make a list that has main ideas for headings. Place the details below the correct main ideas. Your lists should look something like the shopping list on the previous page. Please feel free to shorten the details into notes.

SITUATION A

You have a test for science class tomorrow on animal characteristics. You are required to know the characteristics of *amphibians, mammals,* and *birds.*

You must know which of the characteristics below fits with what kind of animal:

>   feeds young with mammary glands
>   lives in water and on land
>   has wings
>   reproduces by laying eggs
>   reproduces by giving birth to young animal
>   has hair
>   has gill-breathing larvae
>   has hollow bones
>   has backbones
>   has feathers
>   has gelatinous eggs

First write your main ideas. Then organize the list of details in the spaces below. You may use a detail more than once.

MAIN IDEAS: _____   _____   _____

DETAILS: _____   _____   _____

_____   _____   _____

_____   _____   _____

_____   _____   _____

_____   _____   _____

_____   _____   _____

SITUATION B

You have to write a biography about a famous person. You have to answer these questions about the person:

1. What happened in the person's *early years?*
2. What kind of *education* did the person receive?
3. What made this person *famous?*

You choose Abe Lincoln because you already know the following about him: he walked three miles to school each way to get a good education: his mother was Nancy Hanks; he had one sister; his father was Thomas Lincoln; the family moved from Kentucky to Indiana when Abe was young; he went to school to become a lawyer; he could write well; he debated Stephen Douglas; he was a captain in the Black Hawk War; he trained as a store clerk; and he became 16th President of the United States.

First write your main ideas. Then organize your list. Add any other details that you know.

MAIN IDEAS: _____   _____   _____

DETAILS: _____   _____   _____

_____   _____   _____

_____   _____   _____

_____   _____   _____

_____   _____   _____

_____   _____   _____

EXERCISE II

Directions: Read Situation A, and follow the directions at the end of the situation. Do the same for Situation B on page 118.

SITUATION A

Before you can get this week's allowance, your parents insist that you do the following chores:

>   make bed
>   do pages 3-4 in math
>   put away clean clothes
>   mow lawn
>   dirty clothes in the hamper
>   Social Studies report on Alaska
>   clean shelves
>   rake leaves
>   read three chapters of *Island of the Blue Dolphin*
>   wind up hose

In the space below, make lists of all the chores you have to do. Make sure each list has an appropriate main idea for a heading.

MAIN IDEAS: _____   _____   _____

DETAILS: _____   _____   _____

_____   _____   _____

_____   _____   _____

_____   _____   _____

_____   _____   _____

_____   _____   _____

SITUATION B

You are going on an overnight hike with some of your friends. It is your assignment to bring the following items: pancake mix, candles, *Trivial Pursuit,* dried fruit, matches, muffin mix, comic books, powdered eggs, cards, newspaper (for starting fires), cereal, instant milk, powdered fruit juice, "slam" books, doughnuts.

Guess what three things you are in charge of and create your lists in the space below:

MAIN IDEAS: _____   _____   _____

DETAILS: _____   _____   _____

                _____   _____   _____

                _____   _____   _____

                _____   _____   _____

                _____   _____   _____

                _____   _____   _____

TOPICS

A *topic* is broader or larger than a main idea. It can include several main ideas.

EXERCISE III

Directions: Read statements #1 - #4 below, and answer the questions on the lines provided.

1. The topic of Situation A in Exercise I (page 115) might be *Living Things* or *Animals.* Is there any other topic these ideas might fit under?

_____

2. The topic of Situation B in Exercise I (page 116) might be *Presidents,* or *Famous Politicians.* Can you think of any other topic it could be?

_____

3. The topic of Situation A in Exercise II (page 117) might be *Chores* or *Ways to Earn Money.* Can you think of another topic that would fit these ideas?

_____

4. The topic of Situation B in Exercise II (page 118) might be *Scout Trips* or *Hiking Plans.* Can you think of another topic that would fit these ideas?

_____

EXERCISE IV

Directions: Read the lists in #1 below. Create a topic for the main ideas and details in #1, and write it on the line provided. Do the same for #2 and #3 on page 120.

1. FOOD	FAVORS	ACTIVITIES	TO DO
cake	napkins	dance	bake cake
ice cream	honkers	spin the bottle	write invites
"munchies"	place settings	*Trivial Pursuit*	borrow tapes
hamburgers	prizes	egg walk	go shopping
rolls		charades	get permission
condiments			borrow games
brownies			bake brownies

The topic is _____

2. **EARLY YEARS**   **EDUCATION**   **EVENTS LEADING TO FAME**

one of seven   taught by older brother   became leader of Virginia militia

father died when young   no formal schooling   member of the First Continental Congress

favored son   learned surveying   general of Continental Army

raised in Virginia   took over brother's military duties   commander at Valley Forge

took over Mount Vernon at young age   surveyed wilderness of America   defeated British army

The topic is _____

3. **CLIMATE**   **GEOGRAPHY**   **PEOPLE**   **EXPORTS**

wet   mountainous   Celtic   potatoes

mean temp 55° F   island   redheads   whiskey

mild winters   bays   Gaelic   crystal

raw winters   hills   English speaking   lace

snow rare   lakes   black haired blue eyed   dishes

surrounded by:
Atlantic Ocean
Irish Sea
North Sea

The topic is _____

EXERCISE V

Directions: Pick a topic from the suggestions below. Circle the topic. Then in the spaces below, write out *three* lists showing main ideas and details that fit with this topic.

World War II	Mammals	Famous Authors
Famous Women	Automobiles	Famous Politicians
Vacation spots	Schools	Flight
Television	Technology	Agriculture
Pets	Entertainment	Food
Clothing	Careers	20th Century
Plant Kingdom	Books	Explorers

MAIN IDEAS: _____ _____ _____

DETAILS: _____ _____ _____

_____ _____ _____

_____ _____ _____

_____ _____ _____

_____ _____ _____

_____ _____ _____

_____ _____ _____

UNIT XI SUMMARY: ORGANIZING IDEAS

A category name is also a *main idea*. The ideas and information within a category are the *details* of that *main idea.*

Details give more information about or support a main idea.

A *topic* is broader or larger than a main idea. It often includes several main ideas.

The chart below shows how these terms are related.

DETAILS
are part of
MAIN IDEAS
are part of
A TOPIC

or

A TOPIC
includes
MAIN IDEAS
are supported by
DETAILS

UNIT XII: CHARTS — TABLES AND GRAPHS

INTRODUCTION

A picture or a *chart* can often make clear information that would take many words to explain. For instance, if you were studying the structure of a plant cell, it helps to see a picture of a cell as you are hearing or reading about it.

If you were dividing jobs among the members of the Student Council in order to prepare for a dance, you might make a list or a *table* to show who is on the different committees.

In each of these cases, you are using a *chart* — a kind of picture — to help you understand and organize information. A *chart* can be a diagram, a table, or a graph. Charts are arranged so that you can easily understand and use a lot of information.

Look at the chart of the flower below. It tells you at a glance that a flower is made up of four separate parts. It also tells you what the parts of the pistil and the stamen are and where the parts are in relationship to each other. It would take a great many words to explain these things.

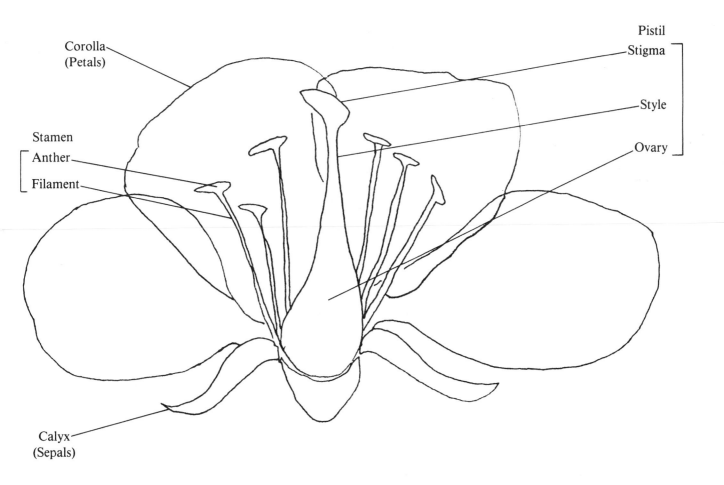

THREE KINDS OF CHARTS

In this unit you will be learning about three kinds of charts: *diagrams, tables,* and *graphs.* You will see how they can help you in these ways:

1. by giving you a "picture" of the information so that the information is easier to *see* and *understand*;

2. by *organizing* the information so that you can find it more easily; and

3. by giving you a way to *compare* data or bits of information.

It is important to understand the kinds of information that diagrams, tables, or graphs present. Then you can use this information to answer questions and solve problems.

EXERCISE I

Directions: Read the paragraphs below about volcanoes. Then answer the questions that follow.

THE BIRTH OF A VOLCANO

A volcano is an opening in the earth's surface through which lava, hot gases, and rock fragments burst forward. Such an opening occurs when melted rock from deep within the earth blasts through the surface. Most volcanoes are atop mountains that the volcanoes themselves have created. These mountains (also called volcanoes) are usually cone-shaped mountains that have been built up by lava and other materials thrown out during eruptions.

The volcano actually begins as *magma,* which is melted rock located deep within the earth. At certain depths within the earth, the temperature is so extremely hot that it partly melts the rock inside the earth. When the rock melts, it produces gas that mixes with the magma or melted rock. Most of this magma forms 50 to 100 miles beneath the surface.

The gas-filled magma gradually rises toward the earth's surface because it is lighter than the solid rock around it. As the magma rises, it forms a large chamber in the crust. The crust is the area between the surface of the earth and the earth's mantle. The magma chamber is the holding place from which volcanic materials erupt. Sometimes these chambers are as close as two miles to the surface of the earth.

1. Where is the magma chamber? _____

2. Which is closest to the center of the earth: the crust, the mantle, or the magma chamber?

    _____   _____

3. How is the cone-shaped mountain formed by volcanic forces?

    _____   _____

EXERCISE II

Directions: Now look at the diagram of the volcano below. First answer questions #1-3, as you did for Exercise I. Then answer #4.

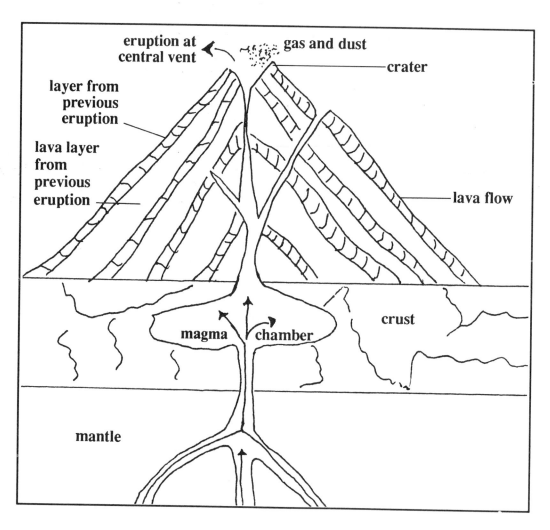

1. Where is the magma chamber? _____

2. Which is closest to the center of the earth: the crust, the mantle, or the magma chamber?

   _____

3. How is the cone-shaped mountain formed by volcanic forces?

   _____

4. Did the diagram help you answer these questions more efficiently? If so, explain how.

   _____

   _____

   _____

TABLES AND GRAPHS: WAYS TO ORGANIZE INFORMATION

Two other kinds of charts are *tables* and *graphs*. Just like the diagram of a volcano, a table or graph can help you understand much information at a glance. Both tables and graphs are carefully organized to present information in a visual way. You must understand the organization in order to use the information in a table or graph.

EXERCISE III

Directions: Now look at the table and the graph below. Although they look different, each is presenting the same information. As you look at this table and graph, try to think of reasons for presenting the information in each way. Then answer the questions that follow on page 129.

TABLE

SPEEDS OF ANIMALS

ANIMAL	MPH	ANIMAL	MPH
cheetah	70	cat	30
lion	50	human	27.89
quarter horse	47.5	elephant	25
cape hunting dog	43	black mumbra snake	20
coyote	43	wild turkey	15
zebra	40	squirrel	12
greyhound	39.35	pig	11
domestic rabbit	35	chicken	9
grizzly bear	30	three-toed sloth	.15

GRAPH

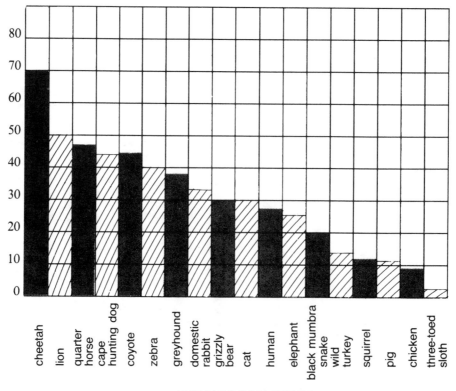

SPEEDS OF ANIMALS

ANIMALS MEASURED

128

1. Which chart would be more useful if you wanted to list more information about the speeds of other animals?

_____

2. Which chart would be more useful to show how impressive the cheetah's running ability was when compared to other animals?

_____

3. Which chart gives more specific information? _____

4. Which chart makes it easier to see that humans have a low average running ability when compared to other animals?

_____

DIFFERENT WAYS TO SHOW DIFFERENT KINDS OF INFORMATION

Tables and different kinds of graphs are organized to show different kinds of information.

For example, the table listing speeds of animals shows you specific information organized by how fast each animal runs. The graph shows you the difference in the animals' running speeds. You get a sense of how much faster one animal runs than another.

In the next four exercises, you will be using four different kinds of graphs to help you see and use information. As you learn about each graph, try to notice the particular kind of information that is best shown by that graph.

EXERCISE IV: BAR GRAPHS

Directions: Read the information about BAR GRAPHS below. Then study the bar graph and answer the questions on page 131.

A *bar graph* shows information by using different length bars to illustrate a certain amount or number of something. Bar graphs are organized on a grid. This makes it easy to compare one thing to another.

Often several different kinds of bars are used, such as in the example below. This makes it easier to see the different aspects of the things being shown by the graph.

The bar graph below shows the results of a poll taken by a Student Council Committee in the Madville School. This committee asked 50 boys, 50 girls, and 50 teachers what their favorite sports were, so that Madville could develop some afterschool sports activities. They put the information in the form of a bar graph in order to make a presentation to the Student Council.

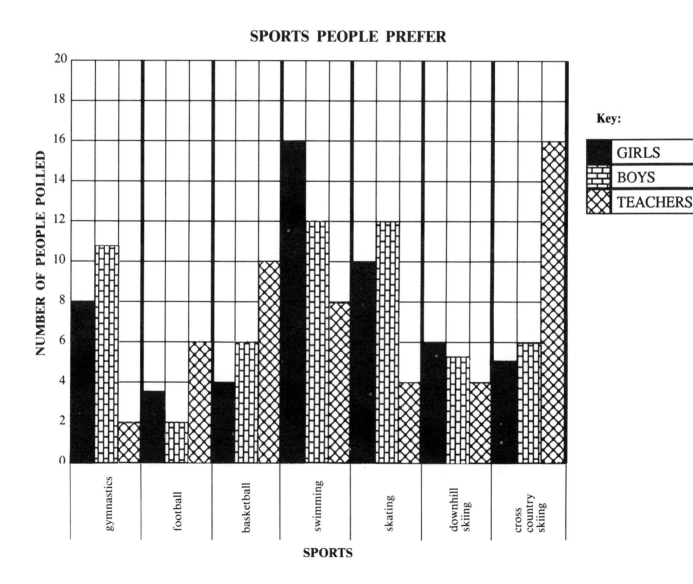

SPORTS PEOPLE PREFER

1. What is the most popular sport at Madville School? _____

    The least popular? _____

2. What sport probably has more girls signing up for it than boys?

    _____

3. Which two populations are the most alike in their choices of favorite sports?

    _____

4. From looking at this poll, there are some indications of the geographical location of the Madville School. Where do you think this school may be located? Why?

    _____

    _____

5. Circle the letter before each of the following ideas that can be represented by creating a *bar graph*.

    a. Number of males and females born in different countries

    b. Percentage of different trees found in a forest

    c. Number of extinct animals found in different countries

    d. How many males and females favor a candidate

    e. How many months with rainfall over three inches

EXERCISE V: PICTOGRAPHS

Directions: Read the information below about PICTOGRAPHS. Then study the pictograph below, and answer the questions on page 133.

A *pictograph* is a kind of chart that uses pictures to represent a certain number of something. In a pictograph, a certain amount of something is shown by a picture so that you can easily see how the amounts relate to each other. Pictographs usually are not exact but show amounts that are "rounded off" to the nearest unit.

In the example below, the pictograph shows how much money the Madville student body has earned toward end-of-the-year school trips. Twelve students worked together with a teacher in groups called Teacher Advisories (TA) to earn money. The chart below shows how much money each TA earned. Each $ stands for ten dollars.

$ TOWARDS CLASS TRIPS

Mrs. Arnold's TA	$	$	$						
Ms. Barwin's TA	$	$	*S*						
Mr. Bolger's TA	$	$	$	$	$	$	*S*		
Mr. Fotion's TA	$								
Mr. Funzula's TA	$	$	$	$	$	*S*			
Mr. Kulhowvick's TA	$	$	$	*S*					
Mr. Rowe's TA	$	$	$	$	$	$	*S*		
Ms. Ryder's TA	$	$	$	$	*S*				
Mrs. Sokolich's TA	$	$	$	$	$	$	$	$	$
Ms. Toesing's TA	$	$	$	*S*					

$ = 10

S = 5

school goal: $1,000

132

1. What TA has earned the most money so far? _____
   Approximately how much more money has this TA earned than its nearest competitor?

   _____

2. How much money has Ms. Barwin's TA earned? _____

3. How much more money has Ms. Ryder's TA earned than Ms. Arnold's?

   _____

4. How much money have the students earned in total? _____
   Approximately how much more money needs to be earned to reach the school's goals?

   _____

5. Circle the letter before each of the ideas below that you think could be easily represented in a pictograph:

   a. Yearly population of US

   b. Number of hours spent on homework per week

   c. Percentage of time doing daily activities

   d. Number of cars sold by a salesperson per year

   e. Spelling test scores

   f. Number of UFO sightings in Milford, Utah

   g. Number of gallons of milk sold by major companies

EXERCISE VI: LINE GRAPHS

Directions: Read the information below about LINE GRAPHS. Then study the line graph below, and answer the questions on page 135.

Line graphs are useful when you want to look at something to see how it changes under certain measurable conditions, such as over time. Line graphs are also useful when you want to look at the development of similar items so that you can compare them. In the line graph below, for instance, you can see how precipitation changes over a period of time. This line graph also makes it easy to compare rainfall with snowfall.

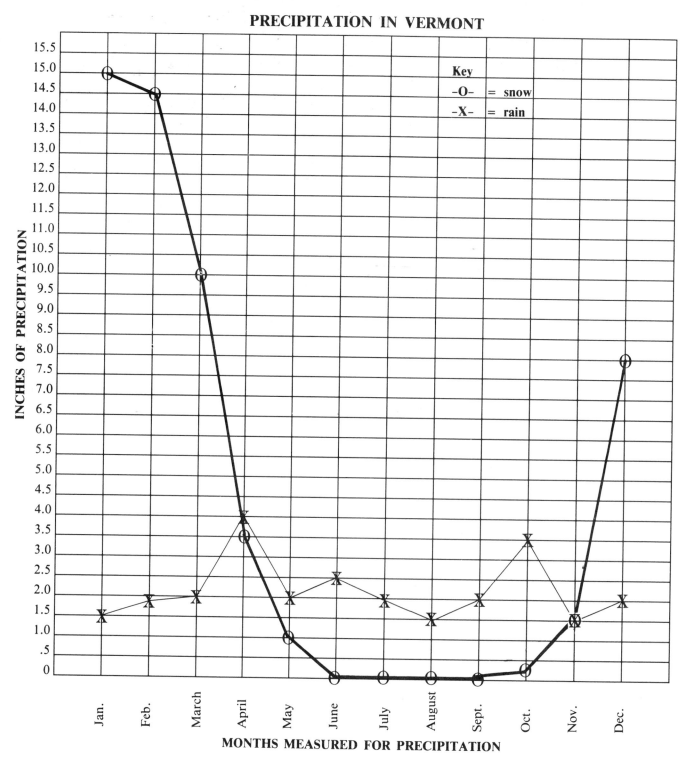

PRECIPITATION IN VERMONT

Key
-O- = snow
-X- = rain

INCHES OF PRECIPITATION

MONTHS MEASURED FOR PRECIPITATION

1. Name four months when there is no measurable snow in Vermont. _____

   _____

2. Name the three months with the most snow. _____

   _____

3. When might it be best to plan a ski vacation in Vermont? Why? _____

   _____

   _____

4. Name the month when it rains and snows almost the same number of inches.

   _____

5. Circle the letter before each of the ideas below that you think could be easily represented by a line graph:

   a. The yearly earnings of three major companies

   b. Sports people prefer

   c. Yearly number of boy and girl graduates from a certain school

   d. The growth of two similar plants under different conditions

   e. The percentage of people with different racial backgrounds living in the same area

   f. The planets in a solar system

EXERCISE VII: PIE GRAPH

Directions: Read the information below about PIE GRAPHS. Then study pie graph below, and answer the questions on page 137.

Below is an example of a *pie graph.* In a pie graph, a circle is used to show the whole amount of something. In the example below, it shows the whole amount of energy sources used in the United States.

The whole is divided into parts that are either fractions or decimals. The parts in this example show what part of all the energy sources are petroleum, natural gas, coal, hydroelectric power, nuclear power, and "other." "Other" shows the combined small amounts of less used energy resources, such as the burning of wood and trash.

A pie graph makes it easy to see the parts of a whole (percentage) and compare them to each other.

SOURCES OF ENERGY CONSUMED IN THE U.S.

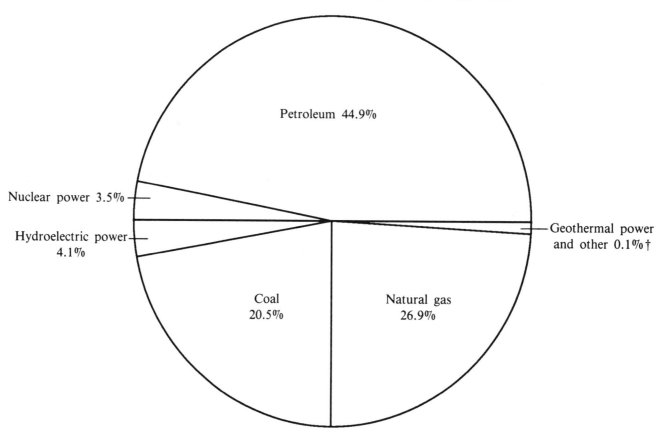

† other includes coke, waste, and wood

1. What are the three most used energy sources in the U.S.? Name them in order from the most to the least. _____

    _____

2. What does "other" include? _____

    _____

3. Which of these energy sources do you consume? _____

4. What does the total circle of this pie graph represent? _____

    _____

5. Circle the letter before each of the ideas below that could be illustrated by a pie chart:

    a. How goods are transported in Canada

    b. Activities that are inexpensive

    c. Speeds of animals

    d. Lists of classmates' birthdays

    e. Number of stars seen from earth

    f. Amount of time spent each day on different activities

UNIT XII SUMMARY: CHARTS — TABLES AND GRAPHS

Charts include diagrams, tables, and graphs. Charts are a good way of showing information. You can learn a great deal just by looking at a chart if you know how to read it.

Each kind of chart can show you different kinds of information:

Diagrams are used to make complicated reading clearer because they *show* you what you are reading about.

Tables show you lists of information, such as who is serving on what committee or the alphabetical list of countries and their populations.

Bar graphs show you information by using different length bars to illustrate a certain amount or number of something. Often more than one kind of bar is used so that you can compare one thing to another.

Pictographs show you information by having a picture represent a certain number of things. For instance, a stick figure could represent 100 human beings. In a pictograph, a certain amount of something is shown by a picture so that you can easily see how different amounts relate to each other. Pictographs usually are not exact but show amounts that are "rounded off" to the nearest unit.

Line graphs show how something changes under certain measurable conditions, such as time. Line graphs are also useful when you want to look at the development of similar items in order to compare them.

Pie graphs make it easy to see the parts of a whole and compare them with each other.

All these kinds of charts can help you to understand and learn important information.

UNIT XIII: USING A DICTIONARY

CHALLENGE!

The dictionary was probably the first reference book that you became familiar with. You already know a lot about using it. The challenge that your teacher is going to read to you will show you how quickly you can locate and use information from the dictionary.

WORD # 1

1. _ _ _ _

2. _____

3. _____

4. _____

5. After dinner tonight, do you want to play *cards*?

   entry _____ definition _____

WORD # 2

1. _ _ _ _ _

2. _____

3. _____

4. _____

5. Please put the ads at eye *level* so everyone who comes into the store can see them.

   entry _____ definition _____

WORD # 3

1. _ _ _ _

2. _____

3. _____

4. _____

5. If you don't *hush* up, the whole town will know your secret.

   entry _____ definition _____

THE DICTIONARY - A COMPLICATED RESOURCE

If you had any trouble with the *Challenge*, don't feel bad. This unit will help you to learn more about how to use a dictionary.

EXERCISE I

Directions: Read sentence #1 below. If what the sentence says is true for you, put a check in the space before the sentence. Do the same for sentences #2-4.

Then answer question #5.

1. _____ I have trouble locating words that I don't know how to spell.

2. _____ I do not use guide words to help locate information.

3. _____ I have difficulty choosing the meaning that fits the context of the sentence.

4. _____ I have difficulty figuring out how a word is pronounced.

5. List any other problems you might have when using a dictionary.

_____

_____

_____

_____

INTRODUCTION

You may have discovered that using a dictionary can be a frustrating experience. You want to learn about the meaning of a word, so you look it up in the dictionary. But, instead of finding one meaning, you find many different ones! What do you do then?

This unit will help you learn how a dictionary is organized and how you can make better use of it.

EXERCISE II

Directions: Look up the word *run* in your dictionary. Read through its many meanings. How many different meanings are listed for the word *run*? Write the number of different meanings in the blank below.

_____

Read the following sentences carefully. Find the best definition for the word *run* as it is used in each sentence below. Write the correct definition on the line under each sentence.

EXAMPLE

"*Run* and call the vet," she ordered. "I can't seem to give her the help she needs with the colt."

_____

1. "I can *run* faster than you." he snarled at me from the starting gate.

   _____

2. She had a *run* in her tights.

   _____

3. The dog was not used to his collar and chain. He used to have the *run* of the whole neighborhood.

   _____

4. She decided to *run* for Attorney General even though a woman had never held that office before.

   _____

5. Even with the critics' praise, the play only had a three month *run* on Broadway.

   _____

6. We wait eagerly for the salmon to *run* each year.

   _____

Continued on page 142.

7. His fingers seemed to fly over the clarinet as he played the *runs* in the sonata with ease.

_____

8. He always liked the Phoenix to Los Angeles *run* with its long stretches of open road.

_____

9. The motorcycle was *run* off the road by a truck.

_____

10. The ship's captain wanted to *run* the blockade, but the admiral overruled his command.

_____

EXERCISE III

Directions: The dictionary lists the meanings of a given word. The dictionary also provides other helpful information about words and how to use them.

On page 143 you can see three dictionary entries for the word *trace*. Some parts of these entries are already named. Look over these parts and their names carefully.

Then on the lines provided, name as many of the other numbered parts as you can. Even if you don't know what a part is called, describe what you think the part is or what it does in the dictionary definition.

1. _____ entry word _____

2. _____

trace[1] / tras / n. **1.** a sign, such as a mark, footprint, track, etc., showing that something has passed by or happened: We found traces of the migrating herds. The outlaws left traces of their overnight camp. **2.** hint or slight evidence: a trace of sorrow. **3.** small amount: There was a trace of mercury found in the tuna. **4.** in psychology, the changing of brain cells set up by repeated events considered to be the physiological foundation of memory. **5.** a mark or some such sign made by an instrument which records: The polygraph trace is designed to show the intensity of the subject's response.

3. _____

_____

_____

4. _____

_____

trace[2] / tras / vb. **1.** to sketch over, drawing by placing a transparent piece of paper over a map, drawing or photo. **2.** to draw with care, i.e., figures or lines. **3.** to review in outline form: We traced the development of the Incas. **4.** to be guided by marks or signs: The hunters traced the wounded deer by following her blood stains. **5.** to show a record of: The polygraph traced the subject's responses. traced. tracing. (from Old French tracier, from Latin tractus, from trahere, "to draw")

5. _____

_____

_____

6. _____

_____

7. _____

_____

_____

trace[3] / tras / n. **1.** either of two straps attached to the animal and a vehicle which is drawn by the animal **2.** LEADER **3.** one or more vascular bundles supplying a leaf or twig. **4.** connecting bar or rod pivoted at each end to another piece to transmit motion from (Old French meaning "traces" from Latin tractus, "a dragging") kick over the traces Informal showing independence or insubordination

8. _____

_____

9. _____

10. Idiom — found in dark

print after the entry. _____

143

EXERCISE IV

Directions: Using the dictionary entries on page 143, write the best meaning for the way *trace* is used in each of the following sentences on the line below each sentence.

EXAMPLE

There are *traces* of arsenic in the dead man's body.

_____

1. He carefully *traced* the treasure map onto the see-through paper.

   _____

2. We found no *traces* of the lost pony.

   _____

3. She looked at the old homestead with a *trace* of regret in her eyes.

   _____

4. The *trace* from the stem to the leaf carries nitrogen that is needed for photosynthesis.

   _____

5. We *traced* the bear tracks to the stream.

   _____

6. The lesson was designed to *trace* the rise and the fall of the Roman Empire.

   _____

7. She examined the graph that the machine had drawn by measuring his heart beat. The *traces* showed possible signs of heart weakness.

   _____

8. The *traces* snapped, and the frightened horse ran off as the wagon rolled to a bumpy halt.

   _____

9. She *traced* her ancestry back to the first Dutch settlers.

   _____

10. A tiny *trace* in the watch had broken, stopping the movement of the hour hand.

    _____

UNIT XIII SUMMARY: USING A DICTIONARY

One word can have many different meanings. You can use the dictionary to learn about the various meanings of a word and to figure out which meanings you need to learn.

The dictionary can also give you other helpful information about a word:

1. how the word is pronounced;
2. the part or parts of speech of the word;
3. examples of how the word can be used;
4. various forms of the word: for example, plural, past tense, and so on; and
5. any special uses of the word.

UNIT XIV: PUTTING A BOOK TOGETHER

INTRODUCTION

Almost every textbook has many different parts other than just the *body* or *text* of the book, that is, the written sections in each chapter. Most of your textbooks have all of the parts listed below:

> Title page, and copyright page
> Table of Contents
> Body or text
> Glossary
> Index
> Bibliography

When you know how to find and use all of these parts, your textbook can become more helpful to you in your learning.

In this unit, you'll learn about the different parts of a textbook by putting a book together. The *body* of the "book" you will put together is actually an article called "Monkey Business."

EXERCISE I

Directions: Turn to page 151, and *survey* the article "Monkey Business."

TITLE PAGE AND COPYRIGHT PAGE

The *title page* is the very beginning of a book. The *title page* tells you the title of the book. It also lists the author and publisher and where the book was published.

The *copyright page* is usually right after the title page. This page tells you who has the right to print the book and when the book was first printed.

EXERCISE II

Directions: (A) Find the *title page* in this study skills *Program*, and locate the following information:

What is the title of this book?

Who is the author?

Who published the book?

Where was the book published?

(B) Find the *copyright page* of this book. Locate the following information:

Who has the right to print this book?

When was this book first printed?

(C) Using the title page and copyright page in this book as a source of information and as a model, make up a *title page* for *Monkey Business.*

TABLE OF CONTENTS

The *table of contents* tells you what you will find inside the book. It lets you know about the main ideas that are covered in the book. The *table of contents* also tells you how many chapters there are in the book and on what page each chapter begins.

You can find the *table of contents* in the front of the book, usually right after the copyright page.

EXERCISE III

Directions: (A) Find the *table of contents* in this study skills *Program*, and examine it.

(B) Read over the "book" *Monkey Business.* Decide what the chapter headings should be, and make a list of these headings.

(C) Create a *table of contents* for *Monkey Business.* Your table of contents should contain chapter titles and pages on which the chapters begin.

GLOSSARY

The *glossary* of a textbook is a lot like a dictionary for that book. It lists words that are new or unfamiliar to most readers and tells you how the words are pronounced, what part of speech they are, and what their meanings are.

The *glossary* covers meanings that are used within that book. It often doesn't list every meaning of a word as a dictionary would.

You can usually find the *glossary* at the end of the body of the book.

EXERCISE IV

Directions: (A) Read the "book" *Monkey Business*.

(B) There are 17 underlined words or terms in the body of *Monkey Business*. Find all of these words or terms; make a list of them, and put the list into alphabetical order.

PLEASE NOTE! A term is a group of words that have a particular meaning together. The terms in *Monkey Business* are animal behaviorists, endangered species, and hurdy-gurdy man.

In a *glossary,* terms like these are listed as if they were a single word.

(C) Using context clues or a dictionary, write a glossary definition for each underlined word or term in the body of the "book." Be sure to use the same meaning that is used in *Monkey Business*.

(D) Put your words and definitions together, so you have a *glossary* for *Monkey Business*.

INDEX

An *index* lists specific names and ideas found within a book. This list is in alphabetical order. Numbers of the pages where ideas and names can be found are listed after the names and ideas.

You can usually find the *index* at the very back of the book. Some reference books have a separate volume for the index.

EXERCISE V

Directions: (A) All of the words and terms in the list below appear in the "book" *Monkey Business*. Put this list of words and terms into alphabetical order.

Pre-monkey	Tree shrew	Bushbaby
Tarsier	New World monkeys	Old World monkeys
Proboscis monkey	Spider monkey	Hurdy-gurdy man
Monkeys as pets	Zoos	Endangered species
Colobus monkey	Guenons	Woolly monkey
Howler monkey	Uakari	Langur
Macaque	Owl monkey	Marmoset
Mangabeys		

(B) Read the "book" *Monkey Business*. As you read, locate the words from the list above in the body of the book. Each time that you find a word in the body of the book, write that page number after the word in the list.

Make sure you find each time that each word appears.

(C) Put all of the words and page numbers together, so you have an index for *Monkey Business*.

BIBLIOGRAPHY

A *bibliography* is a list of references that an author has used to help him or her write a book or article. References can include books or articles.

A *bibliography* lists the references alphabetically by the author's last name.

A *bibliography* is set up in the following way:

Author's last name, First name. *Title.* Place published: Name of publisher, Date published.

You can usually find the *bibliography* just before the index at the back of the book.

EXERCISE VI

Directions: (A) Arrange the references for *Monkey Business* listed below in correct alphabetical order.

(B) Write out a *bibliography* for *Monkey Business.* Be sure that you have punctuated everything correctly.

Whitlock, Ralph, *Chimpanzees.* Milwaukee: Raintree Children's Books, 1977.

Morris, Dean. *Monkeys and Apes.* Milwaukee: Raintree Children's Books, 1977.

Shuttlesworth, Dorothy. *Monkeys, Great Apes, and Small Apes.* Garden City, New York: Doubleday and Company, Inc., 1972.

Leen, Nina. *Monkeys.* New York: Holt, Rinehart, and Winston, 1976.

Annixter, Jane and Paul. *Monkeys and Apes.* New York: Franklin Watts, 1976.

MONKEY BUSINESS

Introduction: A Brief History

At zoos, people often find themselves standing in front of monkey cages. They stare at the intelligent animals that seem curiously like humans. Monkeys can use simple tools, and their hands twist and turn cleverly. Monkeys even seem to have emotions. Actually, monkeys are like humans in another way. They both belong to the same group of *mammals,* as do chimpanzees and apes. This group is called *primates*. All primates have grasping hands or feet, well-developed vision, and relatively large brains.

The primate story began many millions of years ago. A "pre-monkey" known as the *tree shrew* made its appearance on the earth about 70 million years ago. It preferred the high tree tops where it could look down safely upon the giants we know as dinosaurs. It was one of the first mammals. Since it was so tiny, the *tree shrew* was timid. It preferred hiding to fighting. Its clever, long fingers, a brain that was large for its size, and its ability in climbing made the tree shrew a survivor. It still lives today, long after the dinosaurs, on the island of Madagascar (a large island off the eastern coast of Africa).

tree shrew

The tree shrew, the *bushbaby,* and the *tarsier* are some of the animals we call "pre-monkeys." They are like monkeys in many ways, but they aren't as highly developed as monkeys are.

tarsier

Notice the huge, staring eyes. Unlike "real" monkey's eyes, these eyes cannot move within their sockets.

bushbaby

The first of the "real" monkeys emerged about 30 million years ago. Unlike the "pre-monkey," monkeys have eyes that move in their sockets, arms and legs more useful for speedy climbing and running, hands better developed for holding, and a larger and more complicated brain.

Continued on page 152.

Two Classifications

Monkeys come in all sizes, shapes, and colors. But they fit into two large *classifications* or categories. These classifications are Old World monkeys and New World monkeys. They are put into these classifications because of where they are found. Old World monkeys are found in the rain forests of Africa and Asia. They are also found in the islands off these *continents*. New World monkeys are found in the rain forests of South America and Central America. A few can even be found in Mexico. There are many noticeable differences between these two kinds of monkeys.

Old World Monkeys

Old World monkeys are generally considered to have more intelligence than New World monkeys. They will often use simple tools, such as a stick for digging out delicious ants or a rock for killing small game. Their noses are more like human noses than those of New World monkeys are. They are narrow and point downward.

Old World monkeys have 32 teeth, the same as humans have. They have tough protective pads under their *haunches*.

At one time, *animal behaviorists,* scientists who study animal behavior, thought that Old World monkeys were more disagreeable than New World monkeys, Old World monkeys were believed to be more dangerous as they fiercely guarded their *territories*. Modern animal behaviorists disagree. They point to the poor conditions under which the first studies were made. The monkeys were kept in small cages, were not fed proper foods, and often were teased. No wonder the monkeys appeared to be fierce!

New World Monkeys

New World monkeys often have a long and agile tail; most Old World monkeys do not. This tail can be used as another hand for grasping and swinging. These tails are called *prehensile* because of their grasping qualities.

The New World monkeys have broad and round noses. They rely on *instinct* for survival. They rarely use tools as Old World monkeys do. Their bodies are generally longer and slimmer. This makes climbing and traveling through the trees easier. Almost all New World monkeys live in trees. Some Old World monkeys get too heavy to feel comfortable staying high up in the air on slender branches.

Proboscis Monkey

Proboscis means long-nosed in Latin. The bright red head and the long nose of the adult proboscis make it one of the strangest looking creatures in the animal world. The adult male's nose can reach three inches below its chin. Scientists believe this nose could be the sounding board for the long drawn out "honk" or "kee-honk" of the proboscis. The proboscis lives in the rain forests of Borneo, an island in the western Pacific Ocean, and travels through the trees in large, noisy troops.

Proboscis monkey watching from his tree top.

The proboscis is an example of an Old World monkey. It may weigh less than a pound at birth, but when full grown, the male can weigh up to fifty pounds. The female weighs about twenty-five pounds. The proboscis does not have sunken eyes like many monkeys. Its eyes are small, and it seems to look out intelligently. A baby proboscis' nose will start out looking much like any other monkey's nose. As the monkey matures, the nose grows, and the lips draw into a smile. It's almost as if the proboscis knows what a strange looking character it is!

The proboscis eats large amounts of leaves. It also enjoys shoots from mangoes and other fruit. However, it is not an overworked monkey, constantly on the lookout for food. It eats when it wants to. It usually prefers to spend its time lounging on its back or sitting motionless among the tree leaves. The proboscis also enjoys an occasional swim in a tropical river or lake.

Hunters value the proboscis monkey for its rust colored fur. This is one reason why the proboscis is on the *endangered species* list.

Proboscis male-his nose can be three inches longer than his chin!

Spider Monkey

One of the most common New World monkeys is the spider monkey. This monkey gets its name because of its "spider-like" appearance as it moves through the trees at remarkable speeds. Its prehensile or grasping tail helps it to be quick and agile. It uses its tail to climb high into the rain forests of South and Central America and Mexico. The tail can also help the spider monkey grab bits of food as it stretches down from the trees. The end of the tail has a patch of bare skin that is very sensitive. It can pick up a small fruit or a peanut.

The spider monkey usually travels in small bands or groups. However, up to thirty spider monkeys have been seen traveling together. Their voices cut through the rain forest in a high pitched warning yelp. This sounds a lot like many barking terriers.

One of the spider monkey's favorite sports is wrestling. It does not like to swim, even though experiments have shown that it can swim quite well. The spider monkey prefers to hook its long tail on a branch and swing back and forth like a hammock.

The spider monkey is the monkey we picture traveling with the *hurdy-gurdy man*. The traveling musician would play his wind-up organ on the street as his spider monkey begged for coins.

Spider-reaching for delicate bits.

"Hurdy-gurdy" man and his trained monkey.

Continued on page 154.

Monkeys in Captivity

Monkeys don't usually adapt very well as pets. They seem quite happy and sweet when they are young but often grow up to be moody and unpredictable. They bite and spit at times and do cute tricks at other times.

Zoos keep many types of monkeys. These monkeys adapt very well if they have large, clean cages, which also have equipment for climbing and swinging.

Besides having monkeys for people to watch, zoos want to help any monkeys that are an endangered species. Monkeys are hunted for food, fur, pets, and medical research. Also, each year more and more acres of rain forest are being cut down by farmers and builders. Monkey populations all over the world are on the _decline_. Since monkeys _breed_, or reproduce their young, very well in captivity, a well-kept zoo is an important place for them.

Some information about the kinds of monkeys you might find in a zoo is listed below.

Type of Monkey	Zoo Life Span	Home Continent
Colobus monkey	8-12 years	Africa
Guenons	20-30 years	Africa
Howler monkey	10-15 years	Central, South America
Langur	10-20 years	Asia
Macaque	25-30 years	Asia
Mangabeys	15-20 years	Africa
Marmoset	2-8 years	South America
Owl monkey	10-13 years	Central, South America
Proboscis monkey	4-10 years	Asia
Spider monkey	17-20 years	South, Central America
Uakari	5-9 years	South America
Woolly monkey	10-12 years	South America

Perhaps you'll go to a zoo one day. If you do, stand in front of the monkey cage and try to imagine being in the rain forests of South America, Central America, Africa, or Asia. Don't be surprised if you think you see a monkey look right at you and then seem to be laughing. The monkey may just think humans are strange looking creatures!

EXERCISE VII

Directions: Answer the questions below, using the table of contents, the glossary, the index, and the bibliography that you have put together for *Monkey Business.*

1. By looking at the table of contents, can you tell if this book will inform you about what monkeys eat? How do you know?

    _____

    _____

2. Use the glossary to help you answer this question: Can you give an example of an *instinct*?

    _____

3. Use the index to help you answer this question: What is unusual about the "pre-monkey's" eyes?

    _____

    _____

4. Use the bibliography to help you answer this question: Which book is the most recent source of information for *Monkey Business*?

    _____

EXERCISE VIII

Directions: Answer the questions below, using the parts of the "book" *Monkey Business* that you have put together. Then, in the marked space, write which part(s) of the book you used to help you answer the question.

EXAMPLE

What chapter would you read if you wanted to learn about how monkeys live in zoos?

_____

Part of the book: _____

1. Are you a mammal? Name three kinds of mammals

_____

_____

Part of the book: _____

2. Where does the squirrel monkey live?

_____

Part of the book: _____

3. Where are Raintree Children's Books published?

_____

Part of the book: _____

4. What kind of question might you ask an animal behaviorist about your pet dog?

_____

_____

Part of the book: _____

5. Are monkeys good pets? Why or why not?

_____

_____

Part of the book: _____

6. Where would you find a description of the Proboscis monkey?

_____

Part of the book: _____

UNIT XIV SUMMARY: PUTTING A BOOK TOGETHER

You can use your textbooks better to help you learn when you understand how the parts of a book fit together. Also, when you want to find out specific information, knowing the parts of a textbook and how to use them can save you time and effort.

The main parts of a textbook are these:

1. The *title page* tells you the title of the book. It also tells you the author, the publisher, and where the book was published.

2. The *copyright page* tells you who owns the right to print the book and when the book was first printed.

3. The *table of contents* informs you about what the chapters are in the book and on what page each one starts. It can also help you to find out what main ideas are covered within the book.

4. The *body* or *text* of the book includes all of the written sections in each chapter.

5. The *glossary* is like a dictionary for new or unfamiliar words used in the book. Words in a glossary are listed in alphabetical order; each listing tells you the meaning of that word as it is used in the book.

6. The *index* is an alphabetical listing of specific names and ideas found within a book. Numbers of the pages where the names and ideas can be found are listed after the names and ideas.

7. The *bibliography* lists all of the references, the books and articles that the author has used in writing the book.

UNIT XV: STUDYING AND TEST TAKING

INTRODUCTION: STUDYING - FINDING THE RIGHT ENVIRONMENT

Studying means learning. When you are studying to be a musician, a carpenter, or a soccer player, you need the right *environment* for your learning. The *environment* is everything that surrounds you. For example, when you are learning to play a musical instrument, you need a quiet place where you can hear what you're playing and where no one will bother you.

When you are studying for school, you also need the right *study environment*. The first part of this unit will help you to think about what kind of *study environment* is good for you and the way you learn. It will also give you a few suggestions for how you might make better use of your study time.

EXERCISE I

Directions: Read the paragraphs below, and follow the instructions in the third paragraph.

Suzanne's teacher spent the first few days of school talking about the conditions in a good study or learning environment. He said that people have different learning styles and so different people learn best in different kinds of *study environments*. He wanted all of his students to experiment with different *study environments* and find out what helped them to learn better.

Suzanne tried many different conditions before she found the environment that was best for her. Her two most different experiments are pictured on page 159.

Look at the pictures of Suzanne's two study environments. Then, on the lines below, write down all the differences you see.

ENVIRONMENT #1   **ENVIRONMENT #2**

_____   _____

_____   _____

_____   _____

_____   _____

_____   _____

_____   _____

Environment #1

Environment #2

EXERCISE II

Directions: Look at both of the lists you've made on page 158. Circle all of the conditions in both lists that would distract or bother *you* if you were trying to learn.

Now make a list on the lines below of what you would want in an environment that would help you study.

_____

_____

_____

_____

_____

TIPS FOR STUDYING

1. Each person seems to have good times of the day for learning. When do you learn best? In the morning, the afternoon, or the evening? Try to figure out when is the best time for you to study.

2. When you study at home, ask your family to help you by keeping things fairly quiet.

3. Get a small notebook to write down what you have to do for homework. Before you leave school, check your notebook. Then ask yourself, "What will I need to take home tonight?" Make sure you take everything you need home with you.

4. Have your materials together when you start to study. Ask yourself, "Do I need a pencil and paper? A dictionary? Anything else?"

5. How long can you pay attention when you're doing your school work? Experiment to find out. If you can concentrate for fifteen or twenty minutes, plan to study for that long. Then do something active and fun for a few minutes before you start again.

6. Each time that you plan to study, set goals for yourself. These goals should be things that you can really do in the time you have. For example, you may not be able to read an entire book for a book report. Instead, decide how many chapters you can read, and try to reach your goal.

WHAT IS YOUR LEARNING STYLE?

In the *Introduction to Study Skills* you thought about your learning style, or the way you learn best. Some people learn best when they *hear* information. Others learn best by *writing* important details. Sometimes *picturing the facts* is a good way to learn. Another way to learn is to *try to connect* or make sense of how facts fit together. Most of us learn by combining these ways.

When you pay attention to how you learn best, you will be able to learn more effectively.

EXPERIMENT WITH YOUR LEARNING STYLE

EXERCISE III: PART A

Directions:　You will experiment to see how you learn the best. Look at the chart called *Facts About the First Five American Presidents* on page 162. You will have five minutes to try to memorize the facts. Then you will be asked to fill in the blanks on a similar chart.

Think about ways that you learn the best. Try some of the following ways:

1. Say the facts aloud to yourself.

2. Study the lists. Then cover the lists and see if you can remember the information.

3. Write the facts on another piece of paper.

4. Think of the facts in a way that makes sense to you. For example: Of the first five American presidents, three of them were Democratic-Republican. Each of the first five presidents, except for John Adams, had eight years in office. James Monroe was famous for the Monroe Doctrine.

FACTS ABOUT THE FIRST FIVE AMERICAN PRESIDENTS

NAME	WHEN ELECTED	PARTY	FAMOUS FOR
George Washington	1789	None	First President General in revolution
John Adams	1797	Federalist	Helped write the Declaration of Independence First President to live in Washington
Thomas Jefferson	1801	Democratic-Republican	Author of Declaration of Independence Scientist farmer Architect
James Madison	1809	Democratic-Republican	Founder of the Constitution Husband of Dolly Wrote 9 Amendments
James Monroe	1817	Democratic-Republican	Hero of the Revolution Monroe Doctrine

EXERCISE III: PART B

Directions: Now see how many facts you remember. Fill in the blank spaces below. When you have finished, turn back to the previous chart and check your answers.

REMEMBER: This is an experiment to see how you learn; this is not a test. It is more important to recognize how you learn than to pay attention to how many facts you remember.

FACTS ABOUT THE FIRST FIVE AMERICAN PRESIDENTS

NAME	WHEN ELECTED	PARTY	FAMOUS FOR
1. _____	1789	None	First President 2. _____ _____
John Adams	3. _____	Federalist	4. Helped write the _____ _____ First President to live in Washington
5. _____	1801	Democratic-Republican	Author of Declaration of Independence 6. _____ Architect
James Madison	7. _____	8. _____	9. Founder of the _____ 10. Husband of _____ 11. Wrote ____ Amendments
12. _____	1817	Democratic-Republican	13. Hero of the _____ 14. _____ Doctrine

EXERCISE IV

Directions: Look at the statements below. Check the statements that apply to you.

_____ 1. I learn facts best by writing them.
_____ 2. I learn facts best when I see them in lists and memorize what the lists look like.
_____ 3. I learn facts best when I say them aloud.
_____ 4. I learn facts best by combining #1 - #3.
_____ 5. I have a difficult time memorizing facts, but I can remember facts when I see how they all fit together.

INTRODUCTION: TEST TAKING

When you put your time and effort into studying for a test, you want to do well. To do that, you need to learn the material that the test covers. You can also do better on tests if you understand how to answer the different kinds of questions. This part of the unit will suggest some tips you can use with five different types of questions:

true/false questions
matching questions
multiple choice questions
short answer questions
fact/opinion questions

TRUE/FALSE QUESTIONS

True/false questions are statements that you are asked to judge: are they true or false?

Tips for true/false questions

1. Read the question carefully. If *any part* of the statement is false, then it is a false statement. Mark it false.

2. Watch for "key words" like the ones listed below. Think about what these words mean in the statement; they can help you make a decision.

always	all	never
only	usually	often
frequently		

EXERCISE V

Directions: Read the statements below. Decide whether each statement is true or false. Mark a T for true or an F for false in the space before each statement.

_____ 1. All people who live in Norway have blond hair.

_____ 2. Mercury, Venus, Jupiter, Mars, and the Earth's moon are planets within our solar system.

_____ 3. All even numbers can be divided evenly by two.

_____ 4. Plants never grow unless they get direct sunlight.

_____ 5. A calm always comes before a thunderstorm.

_____ 6. Animals usually have their young in the spring.

MULTIPLE CHOICE QUESTIONS

Multiple choice questions ask you to choose the right answer from a group of possible answers.

Tips for multiple choice questions

1. Read the question carefully. Then see if you know the answer to the question *before* you even look at the choices.

2. Read all of the choices given, and pick the *best* answer. Some questions give two or more answers that are right in some way. You need to pick the one that is the *best* answer.

3. Be sure to read *all* of the choices given, even if the first or second one seems right. They may all be correct, and the last choice may be "all of the above."

4. If you don't know which answer is right, cross out all of the ones that you know are *wrong*. Then pick the best answer from the remaining choices. If you don't know which one is best, make a good guess.

5. You should always put down an answer on a multiple choice question, even if it's a guess, unless your teacher tells you not to guess.

EXERCISE VI

Directions: Answer each of the questions below by writing the letter of the correct answer in the blank at the right.

1. The word *watch* means: (A) a timing device (B) to look at something closely (C) a duty on a ship (D) all of the above.

   _____

2. Railroads played an important role in American history because (a) they transported all of the country's supplies (B) they never broke down (C) they were often smelly, so people started taking airplanes (D) they provided efficient transportation for people and supplies.

   _____

3. When Columbus set sail in 1492 (A) the earth wasn't round (B) all people believed that the earth wasn't round (C) Columbus believed that the earth was round (D) almost all of the sailors believed that the earth was round.

   _____

4. Bats are unlike most mammals because they (A) never eat eels (B) have body temperature changes (C) cannot learn to read and write (D) hibernate in the summer when it is the coldest.

   _____

SHORT ANSWER QUESTIONS

Short answer questions ask you to write in the correct answer as part of a statement. They are also called "fill in the blank" questions.

Tips for short answer questions

1. Read the question carefully. Ask yourself: what is this question asking? Then write in the answer if you know it.

2. If you don't know the exact answer but do know something that is related to it, write down what you *do* know. You may get partial credit for it.

3. If you don't know the correct answer but have an idea about it, make a good guess!

EXERCISE VII

Directions: Read the statements below. Fill in the best answer that you know.

1. There are _____ months of the year that begin with the letter "J".

2. The sixth American president was _____ .

3. The three states of matter are gas, solid, and _____ .

4. The author of *The Chronicles of Narnia* is _____ .

5. The United States is bordered by two other countries. The northern border country is

   _____ . The southern border country is _____ .

MATCHING QUESTIONS

Matching questions usually give you two lists of information and ask you to match things on one list with things on the other.

Tips for matching questions

1. Match the easiest things first, the ones you know most about.

2. When you've matched an item, cross out its number or letter, so you know you've already done it.

3. If you're not sure about any of the items, make a good guess!

EXERCISE VIII

Directions: Read the two lists below. Write the number of the piece of sports equipment in the blank before the sport for which you'd use the equipment.

a. _____ baseball   1. shoulder pads

b. _____ football   2. hoop

c. _____ basketball   3. foil

d. _____ field hockey   4. paddle

e. _____ ping pong   5. mallet

f. _____ polo   6. hockey stick

g. _____ fencing   7. bat

FACT/OPINION QUESTIONS

A *fact* is a statement that can be proven to be true or false. An *opinion* is a belief. A belief can not be proven.

Look at the question below:

The United States did not pass the 19th Amendment, which gave women the right to vote, until 1920 because   a) men still wanted women at home to cook and raise families   b) women were not politically wise enough   c) in those times women were not as intelligent as men   d) it took over forty years for enough states to pass the 19th Amendment.

Although you might agree with some of the first three choices, they are really *opinions* and not *facts*. Usually true/false, multiple choice and short answer questions are looking for *facts* and not *opinions*.

Another kind of question asks you to identify statements as *fact* or *opinion*. It is important to know that opinions are not wrong. Opinions can be supported by facts.

Tips for finding facts

1. Facts usually explain who, what, where, or why.

2. Facts can be found in a reference book such as a dictionary, an encyclopedia, an atlas, and so on.

3. Facts are either true or false.

4. The following words are usually *not* found in factual statements.

should	may be	could have been
if	should be	probably

EXERCISE IX

Directions: Read the statements below. Decide whether they are facts or opinions. Write an O before the statements that are opinions and an F before the statements that are facts.

_____ 1. Children should be seen and not heard.

_____ 2. The United States had thirteen original states.

_____ 3. Dancers have a deep appreciation for music.

_____ 4. George Washington was an officer in the Continental Army.

_____ 5. The United States could have been the first country in outer space if more money were given to space exploration in the 1950's.

_____ 6. Abraham Lincoln walked three miles to school.

_____ 7. The earth will probably have a significant climate change in the next ten years.

_____ 8. All people should have a right to equal education.

UNIT XV SUMMARY: STUDYING AND TEST TAKING

Your *study environment* can have a lot to do with how well you learn. Find out what kind of study environment works best for you. Then do your studying in that kind of environment.

Also try to understand how you learn the best, your *learning style*. When you study, use the ways that best help you to learn.

When you understand how different kinds of questions work, you can often do better on tests.

1. True/false questions

    If the answer is only partly false, mark it false. Watch out for "key words" like *always, never,* or *only.* These words can help you decide whether a statement is true or false.

2. Multiple choice questions

    Read the question, and see if you know the answer before you look at the choices. Then read all the choices, and pick the *best* answer. If you're not sure about the answer, cross out the choices that are wrong. Then choose the best remaining answer. Make a good guess!

3. Short answer questions

    Read the statement carefully. If you don't know the exact answer, write down the best answer you can think of.

4. Matching questions

    Match the items you know first. Then cross them out. Make a good guess about the remaining items.

5. Fact/opinion

    It is important to be able to tell fact from opinion. Multiple choice questions and true/false questions are usually looking for facts and not opinions. You can recognize facts as short bits of information that you can locate in a reference book. There are also "key words" that help you decide what are not facts, such as *should be, probably,* and *may be.*

NOTES